THE ONE PERCENT EDGE

Small Changes That Guarantee Relevance and Build Sustainable Success

SUSAN SOLOVIC

WITH RAY MANLEY

AMACOM

AMERICAN MANAGEMENT ASSOCIATION

New York • Atlanta • Brussels • Chicago • Mexico City • San Francisco
Shanghai • Tokyo • Toronto • Washington, DC

To my wonderful friends and family. You make my life rich.

Bulk discounts available. For details visit:
www.amacombooks.org/go/specialsales
Or contact special sales:
Phone: 800-250-5308
E-mail: specialsls@amanet.org
View all the AMACOM titles at: www.amacombooks.org
American Management Association: www.amanet.org

This publication is designed to provide accurate and authoritative information in regard to the subject matter covered. It is sold with the understanding that the publisher is not engaged in rendering legal, accounting, or other professional service. If legal advice or other expert assistance is required, the services of a competent professional person should be sought.

Library of Congress Cataloging-in-Publication Data

Names: Solovic, Susan Wilson, author. | Manley, Ray, 1952- author.
Title: The one-percent edge : small changes that guarantee relevance and
  build sustainable success / Susan Solovic with Ray Manley.
Other titles: 1% edge
Description: New York, NY : AMACOM Books, [2018] | Includes index.
Identifiers: LCCN 2017027592 (print) | LCCN 2017054099 (ebook) | ISBN
  9780814438817 (ebook) | ISBN 9780814438800 (hardcover)
Subjects: LCSH: Organizational change.
Classification: LCC HD58.8 (ebook) | LCC HD58.8 .S648 2018 (print) | DDC
  658.4/06--dc23
LC record available at https://lccn.loc.gov/2017027592

About AMA

American Management Association (www.amanet.org) is a world leader in talent development, advancing the skills of individuals to drive business success. Our mission is to support the goals of individuals and organizations through a complete range of products and services, including classroom and virtual seminars, webcasts, webinars, podcasts, conferences, corporate and government solutions, business books, and research. AMA's approach to improving performance combines experiential learning—learning through doing—with opportunities for ongoing professional growth at every step of one's career journey.

10 9 8 7 6 5 4 3 2 1

FOREWORD

I've always been a bit troubled by the adage credited to Benjamin Franklin instructing that "in this world nothing can be said to be certain, except death and taxes."

While I admit to a degree of trepidation when it comes to challenging the words of one of our most beloved Founders, I cannot help but note that there is a third "certainty" that somehow escaped Dr. Franklin's pen.

Change.

Since Franklin, himself, was one of our most prolific agents of change, it is somewhat surprising that he omitted this third certainty in life. Whether it is the certainty that seasonal change will bring about the life-and-death cycle of leaves on trees or the now unquestionable reality that fast-paced advancements in technology will alter our society on an hourly basis in ways we could not predict, or even imagine: change will constantly shock, please, and, if you are unprepared, it will irritate and devastate.

Given the ubiquitous, unrelenting, and hazardous nature of change, how can it be that people choose to pretend that this particular force of nature is somehow *not* happening all around them every moment of every day?

When we go about the daily business of our personal lives, ignoring the constant that is change will often present difficulties that we have not prepared ourselves to confront. The end result is, more often than not, just "live and learn."

However, if we allow ourselves to remain ignorant of change when it comes to the operation of our businesses, the end result is often something far more devastating than simply chalking one up to experience. Indeed, the result is often more akin to one of the other certainties of life.

Death.

This is where *The One-Percent Edge* comes in.

In this indispensable book, crafted for those operating small and large businesses alike, Susan Solovic alerts you to what should be the number-one rule of success in business, or, for that matter, life in general; if you aren't keeping up with or getting ahead of change, you are likely falling well behind. Somewhere . . . somehow . . . your competitors—including those who see themselves as so far ahead that they no longer view you as a competitor—*are* looking deep into the future and are hard at work inventing what will replace your business's contribution to the world and to your bank account.

But only if you let them.

The bad news is that staying relevant and ahead of the game is not something you can accomplish just by snapping your fingers. By the time you realize there's a problem, it's a good bet that you'll be late to the game, with your business already lagging behind those who seek to do a better job with whatever it is you do. So, the sooner you learn how to cope with changes in and to your business, the sooner you can set things on a course to great success.

The good news is that in *The One-Percent Edge*, Susan Solovic gives you the tools to be both proactive and reactive to the changes your business faces every minute of the day, every day of the year. And that edge is going to be the difference between staying one step ahead or falling tragically behind.

Consider how the Polaroid Corporation changed the world with their patented instant camera, based on the remarkable invention by the company's founder, Edward Land. Launched in 1938, the company successfully innovated its way forward in the world of photography by perfecting the inclusion of a darkroom built right inside the camera. So remarkably successful was the company's innovation that Polaroid was achieving annual revenues of $3 billion by 1991— and think about how much $3 billion was worth back then.

However, rather than stay abreast and ahead of the digital forces, inventions, and changes that were surrounding them, Polaroid elected to sit back and enjoy the spoils of a one-time innovation . . . all the way to their first bankruptcy in 2001.

Polaroid had lost its edge.

Keeping that small edge isn't easy. Often, we're all too aware that we're not keeping pace with the same spirit of innovation that allowed us to create a successful business in the first place. Innovation can easily fall behind as we cope with daily management concerns and the many additional matters that fill our brains and hours as we seek to stay on top of our businesses. We know that innovation is critical to maintaining and growing success, but we can't seem to find the time, inclination, or energy to devote to keeping ahead of change.

That is where the following pages come into play.

While you may think you're simply too busy keeping up with your business to stay ahead of the changes that are constantly coming, I can assure you that staying rooted in the present moment *without* an eye to the future is a sure way to prove Benjamin Franklin right: you may have only death and taxes to look forward to.

But, again, it doesn't have to be that way.

This book will give you the answers you need to stay on top of your business at the same time you're re-inventing it. You will learn how to keep your current orders coming in while anticipating what your customers will want down the road.

Most important, *The One Percent Edge* will guide you in the art of recreation at a time when proactive recreation is more critical to your business's success than it has ever been.

There is no disputing that in today's business world, finding and sustaining just a small edge is a prerequisite for winning.

I think you'll find that *The One Percent Edge* is the roadmap that will guide you to creating that powerful difference for you and your business.

Rick Ungar,
Host of Steele & Ungar, SiriusXM POTUS Channel, and
Sr. Contributor Forbes.com

INTRODUCTION

The End of Business as Usual

Regardless of your company's size or what industry you're in. No matter your revenue performance or the popular awareness of your brand today. Despite how well funded you are or how strong your stock price, right now your business is at risk of becoming extinct.

Only 71 of the original Fortune 500 exist today. Why? Because business leaders—from small and big companies alike—have traditionally relied on past results to manage future growth. In today's global, fast-paced, competitive market, looking in the rearview mirror to manage growth is the beginning of the end. Relying on past performance, business leaders get lulled into a false sense of security and find themselves scrambling when a new competitor, technology, or market shift shakes the business's foundation. Once in this predicament, the likelihood of a successful transformation is minimal.

Over the years, we've seen myriad management programs to assist business leaders in transforming their operations to be more competitive, improve productivity, and increase profitability. I recall sitting in a conference room for days on end, back when I worked as an executive for a Fortune 50 company. The organization was struggling through a Total Quality Management analysis to improve our business results. Afterward, the company went back to business as usual.

The Total Quality Management analysis was cumbersome to apply and, in my opinion, added to bureaucratic rigidity, particularly in the areas of the business I ran: marketing and sales. Every job function needed a workflow analysis to measure productivity and output.

The reason I created the One-Percent Edge process and wrote this book is because I recognize the need for businesses to build innovation into their DNA. And I believe the process should be as fluid and intuitive as possible so teams don't get bogged down in minutiae. Agility, creativity, and flexibility are the cornerstones. Let's face it: The five-year strategic plan is a dinosaur. Successful businesses must operate in real time. They must be agile and adaptable, willing to experiment and adjust quickly if needed. Employees should be empowered and emboldened to speak up with creative ideas and concepts. Technology should be leveraged to increase productivity and enhance the customer experience both externally and internally. Financials and metrics need to be reviewed regularly with an open mindset so leaders can make timely business decisions affecting growth.

Most important, to remain relevant and competitive, business leaders must be willing to look at every aspect of their organizations objectively. You need to be prepared to ask the really tough questions. No sacred cows. That means no egos at the table.

The bottom line: If it ain't broke, fix it anyway. No business can rely solely on today's competitive advantage. It's fleeting. When you're on top is exactly the time to ask yourself, "What's next?" Don't wait until it's lying in pieces on the ground. Instead, extend that competitive advantage incrementally.

The process is ongoing. It won't deliver the results you want by going through it one time and marking it off your list. It's a disciplined approach that should become part of your business operations to ensure your ongoing relevancy and success. You can create and maintain positioning as a market leader by constantly reevaluating your value proposition and implementing incremental enhancements throughout your organization.

Adopt the One-Percent Edge process and you're on your way to achieving sustainable success.

Why Businesses Are Failing

In today's crazy, chaotic, fast-paced world there is one truism you can count on: No business is too big to fail or too small to succeed. Change is happening faster than many of us can adapt to. Just when you think you're on top of new trends and technologies, they become old news.

I was invited to give the commencement address at my hometown high school nearly thirty years ago. During my remarks, I told the graduates that in order to succeed they would need to be able to see the future. At the time, I had no idea how accurate that prediction would be.

Of course, no one has a crystal ball, so in order to stay in front of the curve you need to be willing to try new things, fail and learn from the information you've gathered. Marching in place means you're actually moving to the rear and your business is at risk of becoming irrelevant. I believe Sam Walton said it best, "Do it. Try it. Fix it."[1]

Business leaders today need open-minded thinking, not a closed mindset. At this very moment, whether your business is just getting started, struggling to grow, or established and successful, it's on the verge of failure. Every business in this fast-paced, competitive market is at risk. Some will survive; others will disappear from the landscape.

Why? There are many reasons, but in general terms, it's because of an inability to shift as market demands change. Think about the brand names you knew when you were growing up. Personally, I remember the Montgomery Ward catalog store on the courthouse square in my small, rural hometown. What a delight it was to pick up a package of goodies ordered from its big, glossy catalog or to visit one of its retail stores in a larger downtown location. I'm sure many of you don't even remember the Montgomery Ward brand. The company's rivals, such as Sears & Roebuck and J.C. Penney, shifted their focus to suburban retail malls as demographics changed, but by the time Montgomery Ward followed suit, it was too late.

When one company successfully transitions during times of change and others don't, it doesn't mean that one leadership team is smarter or better informed than the others. However, it does reflect on how the organization's leadership reviews, analyzes, frames, and executes under the circumstances. According to authors Matthew S. Olson and Derek van Bever's book *Stall Points*, once a company runs up against a major stall in its growth, it has less than a 10 percent chance of ever fully recovering.

When the leadership finally wakes up to find lost market share and tanking sales, it scrambles to react. The battle cry is, "Change or die." At this point, many managers will begin throwing everything at the wall and hoping something sticks. (Think RadioShack, as I'll explain shortly.) But generally, it's too late to save the ship from sinking, which may result in bankruptcy, acquisition, or default and liquidation.

Here are some of the reasons businesses get derailed:

- Bureaucratic thinking
- Failure to seize a window of opportunity
- Failure to understand the target customer
- Failure to truly listen to the customer
- Failure to understand what motivates the customer
- Inability to cut dead weight
- Too tied to current relationships
- Too much time selling rather than problem solving
- Too focused on the bottom line to adjust to new market trends
- Failure to analyze data in a new framework
- A culture mired in the status quo process

CONTENTS

- Leaders married to the product or service
- Failure to identify niche markets
- Failure to appropriate funds effectively—throwing good money after bad
- No clarity or focus on numbers and key indicators
- Myopic focus on existing competitors
- Failure to recognize obsolescence of product
- Jumping on the bandwagon too late
- If it ain't broke don't fix it
- Effort to compete on price alone
- Disengaged workforce
- Negative company culture

This is not by any means an exhaustive list, but I think you'll see that the main culprit is an inability to let go of "tried-and-true" methods in order to grow the business in a new, more dynamic way. Even in companies where the leadership touts innovation, it's often only rhetoric. When the landscape begins to change, they wait too long. Successful companies today have innovation built into their DNA. That's the premise behind the One-Percent Edge process, which every company can incorporate into its operations to become agile and remain relevant in today's market.

In the following chapters, I'll walk through the process and explain how you apply it to every aspect of your business: product, pricing, people, process, distribution, marketing, etc. When the process becomes a part of your business operations, you'll find yourself on the forefront of your industry. With the One-Percent Edge, your company will be able to shift in a timely fashion and remain relevant in a changing market.

Innovation doesn't necessarily mean launching the next cool, sexy product. In fact, that can be a sure path to the business graveyard. Pet rocks. Cabbage Patch Kids. Rubik's Cube. We've all witnessed the one-hit wonders and the shooting stars that burn out as quickly as they ignite.

When your business has the One-Percent Edge, the market has a reason to remain loyal to you or to change its buying habits. Think of it this way: At 211 degrees, water is hot. But one degree higher and it's boiling. Time to turn the heat up on your business.

Before we begin with the tactical aspects, let's examine some case studies that exemplify missed opportunities and company leadership that failed to appropriately track competition, renew its capabilities, and build and nurture a team or talent. As we discuss these, keep in mind a few key principles of the One-Percent Edge process:

- Innovation doesn't mean disruption.
- Small adjustments can produce major results.
- Differentiation is critical.
- No need to throw the baby out with the bathwater; core competencies reign supreme.
- Change for change's sake is not the answer.
- You can put lipstick on a pig, but it's still a pig.
- Following historic data and strategies is a death knell.
- Business isn't a dictatorship. Listen.
- Embrace creativity.
- Keep your eyes wide open with a 360-degree perspective.
- Embrace technology.
- Learn constantly.

Why the Leader in Instant Photography Went Belly-Up

Some of you may be old enough to remember the original Polaroid cameras. For the first time, you could snap a picture and watch it develop right in front of your eyes—no need to take film to the store for development. Edwin Land, Polaroid's founder, pioneered a process in which colored dyes were passed from a negative onto film inside a sealed unit. Introduced to the market in the late 1940s, Polaroid was a household name by the 1970s.

Instant photography gave an exciting jolt to the status quo. One could easily envision it as a precursor to the digital photography environment. Unfortunately, as well positioned as the company was, it failed to recognize the implications of digital photography in a timely manner. Peter Post, CEO of Cossette Post, a division of the Canadian marketing firm Cossette Communications Group, noted, "Polaroid could have been a major force in digital photography today if somebody had looked out into the culture and tried to figure out where the brand would fit in. They just never went there."

In 2001, Polaroid filed for bankruptcy and has since tried to re-invent itself, even going so far as to hire Lady Gaga as its creative director. Her biggest contribution? Introducing a new group of products called Grey Label. The products included the GL20 Camera Glasses with a built-in camera and dual LCDs, which appeared for playback when wearing the oversize shades. Grey Label was announced at the 2011 Consumer Electronics Show in Las Vegas. Have you heard of these unique camera glasses? I doubt it. They had their fifteen minutes of fame before fading into oblivion. Even the provocative, trendsetting Lady Gaga, with a social media following in the millions, couldn't convince the market that these glasses were a must-have.

Lesson learned: Don't bury your head in the sand. Times are changing. As a business leader, you need to be agile and visionary enough to change with them. Companies that don't respond in a timely fashion scramble to make up ground but usually fade into oblivion. Playing catch-up is not a winning strategy; you can put lipstick on a pig, but it's still a pig.

Products Change and So Do Competitors

In coming chapters, I'll discuss the importance of competitive analysis and how to do it effectively and affordably using today's technology. However, with the One-Percent Edge process, you'll develop skills to identify competitors who might not yet be apparent. I've frequently heard business leaders say they really don't have any competition for their products or services. Trust me: That is never the case. You may not be aware of the competitive forces, but somewhere out there, an entrepreneurial visionary is developing a product in his garage that could wipe you off the map.

An excellent example is Xerox Corporation. Founded in 1906, Xerox leaped into the spotlight in 1959 when it introduced the Xerox 914, the first plain-paper photocopier. Its simplicity attracted a large market, and sales soared to over $500 million by 1965. (In today's dollars, that would be more than $3.7 billion.) It continued to make innovative advancements in the field of photocopying, and it successfully fought off infringements in its core market by IBM and Kodak, both viewed as its primary competitors.

However, while Xerox focused on its domestic competitors, newcomers from Japan— Canon and Ricoh—were pecking away at the market, targeting small businesses and individuals. Once Xerox recognized the magnitude of the situation, it launched a formidable attack on the Asian companies, stemming the tide. But the story doesn't end there. Because the company was focused on stopping the bleeding, its management lost sight of the emerging personal computer market. You might not know this, but Xerox created what is considered to be the first true personal computer, the Xerox Alto, in 1973. And in 1981, the company released a similar system that was the first to incorporate technology such as a bitmapped display, window-based GUI (graphic user interface), mouse, Ethernet networking, file servers, print servers, and email. But the management team didn't see its sales potential. According to Steve Jobs, "They just had no idea what they had."[2] Apple bought rights to the Alto GUI and adapted it into a more affordable personal computer aimed toward the business and education markets. In 1984, Apple released the Macintosh, the first personal computer to popularize the GUI and mouse.

Lesson learned: Don't be blindsided by your competition. Use a 360-degree perspective to analyze the competitive landscape so a counterattack doesn't take your focus off other market opportunities. And never discount a newcomer. The more complacent your company becomes, the easier it is for an upstart to sweep the market. The cemetery for failed companies is filled with businesses that laughed off a new market entrant. The engraving on a headstone reads: "If I had it to do over again . . ."

If It Ain't Broke, Fix It Anyway

During my early childhood years, Firestone was a name synonymous with quality tires. I remember my dad talking about the need to put Firestones on our personal cars and the ones he used in his business.

The company, based in Akron, Ohio, had a fairly simple view of the market: The top U.S. auto dealers were its customers, and its competitors were all the other U.S. tire manufacturers. Strong relationships with customers and employees characterized the company's culture. And the company's strategic growth plan was to keep up with the growing demand for tires in the market. Things were going well for the business, so why tinker with success?

Enter the Michelin Company, a French manufacturer that introduced the radial tire to the U.S. market. These tires were safer, longer lasting, and more economical than traditional tires. Before entering the U.S. market, Michelin had dominated the European market; it soon did so in the United States as well.

The leaders at Firestone were well aware of the new tire technology, so they took quick action, investing nearly $400 million in radial production. However, although quick, their action was not effective. The company tried to force fit new tire production into its old production methods, which didn't work well. Additionally, it continued to produce the traditional tires even though the writing was on the wall that they would soon become obsolete. A failure to close down the old plants and move to efficient manufacturing processes for the radial tires resulted in Firestone burning through a significant amount of cash before ultimately being acquired by Bridgestone, a Japanese company.

Lesson learned: Don't rest on your laurels. Hanging on to the status quo—your current business model—in light of clear market changes is doomed to fail. Although Firestone enjoyed decades of rapid growth, its failure to recognize the need to shift its thinking resulted in the death of a major company. If it ain't broke today, it very likely will be tomorrow. Be creative and get ready for change.

Throwing the Baby Out with the Bathwater

Many of you may remember RadioShack. Originally, these retail stores were home to the latest electronic equipment. They catered to ham radio operators and rode the wave of the CB radio craze in the 1970s. (Remember *Smokey and the Bandit?*) If you wanted to do a DIY electronic project, RadioShack was the place to go. RadioShack was known for its knowledgeable associates, and DIY enthusiasts became a core customer constituency.

RadioShack actually mass-produced a personal computer, the TRS-80. It was a big hit in the market, but the company failed to leverage the opportunity. As new competitors entered the PC market, RadioShack's hardware business ceased to be profitable because it failed to keep up with the changing marketplace.

Trying to find a substitute for the once lucrative PC business, the company jumped on the cell phone craze; it began negotiating commission deals with manufacturers and wireless providers. Consumers flocked to the RadioShack stores to purchase their cell phones and sign up for provider plans, which took about forty-five minutes per customer. As a result, the company's core customers, the DIYers, became frustrated because of a lack of service and took their business elsewhere.

As one might anticipate, the cell phone providers began cutting out the middleman and opened their own stores, leaving RadioShack searching once again for a strategy to establish its footing. A late effort to enter the e-commerce market proved unsuccessful, and a hodgepodge of what some consumers referred to as a weird inventory mix coupled with aggressive sales tactics pushed most customers away from the struggling retailer. All of these failed strategies left RadioShack management no choice but to file for bankruptcy.

Could RadioShack make a comeback? Its core customers, the DIYers, have found other sources for their power connectors and HDMI cables. However, I believe in never saying never. So stay tuned.

Lesson learned: It's important to understand who your target customers are and what they are actually buying from you. In the case of RadioShack, its core customers came not just to purchase electronic trinkets but also to learn from the advice and assistance of store representatives. As the company jumped into new businesses, its sales representatives didn't have the knowledge base to assist those core customers, which resulted in the base going elsewhere. (Later I'll discuss the antithesis to this scenario, the survival of Ace Hardware.)

What These Case Studies Mean to Your Business

I've shared these examples with you so you can see that no matter how large, successful, or strong your business is, it can fade into oblivion quickly in today's market. As a leader, you don't want to wake up one day to the realization that your business environment has changed so dramatically that you feel the need to take dramatic measures to claw your way out of a commercial abyss.

Take a look around you. Without being mired in the day-to-day operations of other businesses, what do you see happening? Do you see market changes that companies aren't effectively responding to?

Think about department stores. How many have closed in the past year or so as online shopping has begun to dominate? What about the media industry? Look at the way newspapers are trying to survive in today's digital market. Even television networks are feeling the effects of digital media. Consumers are now driving the consumption of media on their own terms—when and where they want it—rather than being held hostage to scheduled releases.

What is happening in your industry? Are you focused on the horizon and poised to move quickly and appropriately to remain relevant?

Going forward, I'll give you a process whereby you can begin to evaluate and design a plan of action with agility and foresight. Your business model will have innovation and creativity built into its DNA. Its elasticity will allow you to move quickly and adroitly to implement timely strategies.

Next up, in chapter 1, I'll discuss each step of the process. In subsequent chapters I'll show you how to apply this process to every aspect of your business, from your product to your people to your pricing and process. Innovative companies are constantly enhancing their businesses incrementally—no dramatic swings required—for a One-Percent Edge.

What Used to Work

Here is your call to action. It's a new day and a new way of doing business. Remember, to remain relevant you can't rely on today's competitive advantage; therefore, long-term strategic planning is history. You can create and maintain positioning as a market leader by constantly reevaluating your value proposition and implementing incremental enhancements throughout your organization. Adopt the One-Percent Edge process and you're on your way to achieving sustainable success.

The process can reignite your passion and reenergize your business's growth. In today's rapidly changing marketplace, successful businesses, large and small, must be innovative, agile, and flexible.

CHAPTER 1

Achieving the One-Percent Edge

M. A. Rosanoff: "Mr. Edison, please tell me what laboratory rules you want me to observe."

Thomas Edison: "There ain't no rules around here. We're trying to accomplish somep'n!"

The most important thing to remember about achieving the One-Percent Edge in your business is that it's not the result of a one-time overhaul. To stay relevant and competitive, you need to look at change as a constant. You have to adapt, be agile, and learn constantly.

The key to the One-Percent Edge process lies in a series of questions:

- Are we giving the market a reason to change its buying habits?
- Are we using the right tools and resources to work smarter, not harder?
- Are we constantly enhancing the customer experience?
- Are we looking beyond the horizon for new opportunities and unmet needs?
- Have we articulated a strong vision?
- Do we have an empowered team?
- Are we open to change?
- Do we have a strong company culture?

If the answer is yes, to these questions, then you're moving in the right direction. If it's no or maybe, then keep working on defining your edge. Throughout this book, as you review every aspect of your business, we'll ask key questions like these.

In subsequent chapters, I'll review various aspects of your business where you need to apply the One-Percent Edge process. Once you know the steps involved, I'll provide some thoughts to help you develop questions, strategies, and business approaches. For each business area, the process must be applied completely. No group, department, product line, or process should be excluded. Each element of your business is dependent on the others, and each must be agile and flexible, making use of the right resources.

As part of the process, we'll look at all aspects of your business:

- Leadership
- Customer base
- Products and services
- People
- Marketing
- Processes and Systems
- Finances

A chapter is devoted to each of these seven critical topics. Continually fine-tuning and innovating in all of these areas determines your ability to achieve and maintain the One-Percent Edge.

To achieve the edge, it's your job to ask those questions and apply the process in all seven areas of your business. That is the blueprint that will propel you from just another player in your business sector to the undisputed leader.

Here are the steps in the process:

1. Ask the tough questions.
2. Select and prioritize.
3. Create your action plan.
4. Execute.
5. Measure and review.
6. Repeat.

Business leaders often get lulled into a false sense of security. The One-Percent Edge process is counter to that way of thinking. When you're on top is precisely when you need to begin to position your business for change. Amazon.com CEO Jeff Bezos says it takes five to seven years before the seeds his company plants—things such as expanding beyond media products, working with third-party sellers, and going international—grow enough to have a meaningful impact on the business. That's why the process is ongoing.

As you read about the steps in the process, you can begin to imagine how you could apply them to each of the seven aspects of your business.

Step 1: Ask the Tough Questions

An important aspect of the process is asking the right questions and listening openly to the answers. Business leaders often get stuck in a psychological trap by concentrating on what made them successful, but they fail to recognize that the market is changing. The new buzzword for that is Uberization—referring to the disruptive nature of the transportation app that has forever changed the taxi industry.

You have to ask the really tough questions, the ones you don't know the answers to but need to be asked. You don't know what you don't know, and it's what you don't know that may be the death of your company.

To get started, you must remove yourself from your business's day-to-day operations. When you are caught up in the fray or the daily stresses, it's impossible to lift your head high enough to gain a clear vision about what is happening with your company, your market, and your industry.

We are all taught to be linear thinkers who make decisions according to historical data and experience. In school, we memorize material, take a test, and move on. There is little leeway for creativity based on traditional teaching methods. So it's no wonder that as business leaders and decision makers we resort to the methodology with which we grew up. As Stanford University professor and prominent science educator Paul Hurd said, "Too many facts, too little conceptualizing, too much memorizing, and too little thinking."[1]

Linear thinking doesn't foster a framework for innovation. Creative people may not have answers, but they habitually question the status quo and think about alternatives and improvements. They discover and invent possible answers. They habitually ask better questions.

To build innovation into your company's DNA you need to let go of the old way of thinking and decision making. You must be willing to reframe the questions in order to find innovative solutions. Eight-five percent of C-suite executives say their companies struggle with diagnosing problems. The status quo isn't a choice. The momentum of your business success may carry you through for a period of time, but it won't sustain you. If you sit for too long, your business may begin to die.

Question every aspect of your business. Success is a fickle creature. Don't be lured into complacency. When you're at the top of your game is when you need to work even harder to make sure you remain in that position. So leave your ego at the door.

I always tell people who are in conflict that there are three sides to every story: theirs, the other person's, and the truth. For every situation there is always another perspective, which is why you need to develop the ability to look at things in different ways.

A structured diagnostic analysis will actually impede creative thinking. You need to reframe the questions, but it takes time and practice to develop this skill. Ask questions with a near childlike curiosity. It may feel uncomfortable and even out of control at times. Eventually issues and opportunities will emerge so you can address them in a timely fashion. Too often managers and leaders turn a blind eye to the reality of a situation by rationalizing results or failing to drill down into operational data. One of my mother's favorite sayings was, "Figures lie and liars figure." Data can be used to explain away business declines. An economic downturn, inclement weather, or higher interest rates all can be considered excuses for lagging results. That's why reframing the situation is crucial for transformational results.

Look at what other industries are doing that's innovative and creative. Is there something you can glean from them that could apply to your operations? Pay attention to the businesses you admire most. What is it you like about them? Are those attributes adaptable to your industry? You may be surprised to find that a strategy your local coffee shop incorporated into its business could be a boon for your company too.

For example, when a Ritz-Carlton customer asks for assistance, the response is always, "It's my pleasure." That simple phrase sets the brand apart from its competition and has earned the company numerous awards for customer service. Think about how your front-line employees might impact your business if they began to use that phrase instead of "no problem." ("No problem" drives me crazy, by the way.)

Develop systems and habits that help you keep up to date with innovations in your industry and beyond. Sometimes you can see something that is working in another industry and apply the same principles to yours. This will help you grow your business as well as find new ventures that might threaten it in the future.

For example, in the introduction I discussed the demise of Polaroid, but now I'd like to give you, as the legendary broadcaster Paul Harvey used to say, "The rest of the story."

Despite the fact that Polaroid hit a brick wall with its original product line and couldn't find anything to replace it, the idea of instant cameras did not die...well, not completely.

Today, instant cameras using essentially the same technology as the original Polaroids are enjoying new popularity. In fact, one of the best-selling items in Amazon's camera and photo category is a Fujifilm version of the Polaroid instant camera. Also, Polaroid itself is selling new versions of its old cameras.

You see, sometimes you can be an innovator by introducing an old idea to a new generation. Have you noticed the popularity of Hula-Hoops among millennials? I had a Hula-Hoop in the fourth grade, and today I have a weighted one I use for exercise to build my core muscles. Sometimes old can be new again, with just a One-Percent Edge.

There are also excellent websites you can mine for new and innovative ideas, including crowdfunding sites like Kickstarter and Indiegogo. Another good resource is Product Hunt. Surf these sites about once a week to see if there are any ideas you can adapt to your own business, if someone is working on a business that your company might support, or a new idea is being developed that could cut into your business. Of course, be careful not to infringe on someone's intellectual property.

Read and Learn

"I read a lot of things," says Tess, Melanie Griffith's character in the movie *Working Girl*. "You never know where the big ideas could come from."

Just like looking toward other industries, you may find some of your best ideas come from unexpected places. Exposure to new thinking broadens your horizons and equips you with resources to give you new perspectives. Personally, I'm not a sports person, but reading the sports section of the newspaper or a sports-related magazine often triggers a new idea for my own business.

Plus, as they say, knowledge is power. In the case of a rapidly changing market, learning new things as an individual and as a company opens your mind to new horizons. As part of my One Percent Edge Podcast series, I've interviewed numerous thought leaders on the concept of change. You can subscribe to the program on iTunes. Many of them are addicted to adventure. They climb mountains, hike through jungles, and jump from airplanes. Each experience provides them with new perspectives on life, stimulating their creativity.

Leverage Creativity Exercises

Innovation can never flourish in an organization that's afraid to be a little "out there." You need to build an environment where anything goes. There is no such thing as a crazy idea, whether in regard to a new product or service or your workflow.

Improvisation can be a good icebreaker for creativity. There are companies that specialize in helping facilitate this, or you can have a little fun and give it a try yourself. In a course I taught on creativity, I would throw a mix of crazy items—doggie house slippers, a wooden spoon, earmuffs, a wrench, a printer cartridge, toothpaste—into a bag and segment the class into teams. Each team got to choose one item. The assignment was to brilliantly pitch the item as a new business product without discussing it beforehand. The team members drew numbers to see who would speak first, then the others had to expand on the first idea. It was hilarious, and it got everyone's creative juices flowing.

Improvisation gives your team an opportunity to collaborate, think on their feet, and build on one another's ideas. You never know what will pop up out of the blue.

According to Tom Yorton, CEO of Second City Works, the business-solutions division of legendary comedy training school Second City: "So much of business—like life itself—is one big act of improv. People make plans but, if they accept that there's a whole bunch of stuff they can't control, then most of what they're doing is improvising."[2]

My friend William Donius has written a book called *Thought Revolution* that could unlock your creativity and help you view your business in a new perspective. It's a simple process that begins with moving your pen from your dominant hand to the other. Donius said writing with your nondominant hand activates the right side of the brain and opens you up to creative solutions, giving you the ability to see new ways through problems in your business, career, relationships, health, and spiritual life.

In the book, he explains the science behind this theory and teaches you how to incorporate the technique into your business and your life. Thought-provoking, easy-to-do exercises and prompts show how to connect more fully with your subconscious right brain to help you reduce stress, discover your hidden talents, heal from trauma, and come to a deeper spiritual awareness.

Create a Workspace Conducive to Creativity

Does your work environment inspire innovative thinking? It's a question not many business leaders consider. When I started my Internet business, we rented space in an old building that needed a lot of TLC. We used card tables and borrowed chairs. It was inexpensive, but I really hated working there. Everything felt dirty and old; I'm sure it affected our team's mood. When we moved to a newer building—brightly painted, with lots of light and proper desks and chairs—it was energizing! You could feel the team's morale lift.

What kind of office setting sparks the most creativity? According to research by staffing firm The Creative Group, it depends on the nature of your business. When asked what the ideal work environment is for on-the-job innovation, the top response among advertising and marketing executives was an open-concept space. Employees, however, seem to prefer more alone time, with a private office being the most popular option.

"Different tasks call for different work environments," said Diane Domeyer, executive director of The Creative Group. "Office design should be closely tailored to an organization's needs and a team's primary duties. The main goal for employers should be to create a space where staff members feel comfortable and engaged, and can perform at their best."[3]

Here are a few ideas offered by The Creative Group for crafting a more stimulating work environment:

▶ **Construct creativity zones.** Designate a few areas in the office for brainstorming and impromptu meetings. Stock each space with industry publications and an easel pad to jot down ideas.

▶ **Offer private sanctuaries.** While open floor plans can increase collaboration among employees, some projects require greater focus and concentration.

▶ **Include workstations.** Provide places where individuals can work in solitude without distraction.

▶ **Think outside the office.** Hold team meetings in a nearby park, courtyard, or café. A change of scenery is sometimes all it takes to spark the imagination.

Step 2: Select and Prioritize

"The difference between successful people and very successful people is that very successful people say 'no' to almost everything."

—WARREN BUFFETT

Selecting and prioritizing strategies is probably the most difficult part of the One-Percent Edge process. The dictionary defines *priority* as "a thing that is regarded as more important than another." Strictly speaking, you can't have ten priorities. That would force you to ask the question, "Which of these is more important than the others?" You can have more than one goal, but only one can be the most important.

If you're unable to determine your organization's most important goal, don't expect your team to all be rowing in the same direction. Therefore, to solve the herding-cats problem, you need to have a very short list of goals for your team.

Start with a simple list of the changes you can make and the opportunities you've identified. Don't rule anything out. There is no such thing as a bad idea. However, keep in mind, change for change's sake is never the answer, just as growth for growth's sake can be problematic. Faced with a downturn or diminishing market, many companies get into trouble by acquiring other businesses as a lifeline. Acquisitions aren't necessarily bad, but they must be managed in a controlled way. Cultures and values need to be aligned. Synergies between the businesses should exist.

Many years ago I worked for ITT Corporation. The *Los Angeles Times* once referred to the company as "a global hodgepodge that at times has owned everything from Wonder Bread to Avis rental cars." During my tenure, the company acquired Madison Square Garden. It was hard to describe ITT because of its diverse businesses. Eventually, because of a heavy debt burden, then-CEO Rand Araskog began selling off various entities, but it wasn't enough. Unable to define its direction and with operational leaders who weren't equipped to manage the various operations, the company announced in June 1995 that it was splitting itself into three publicly traded firms. One analyst referred to it as a watershed event in corporate America.

The *Times* noted, "ITT's breakup is further evidence that the gigantic conglomerate—so fashionable in U.S. business during the 1960s and '70s—is largely a dinosaur today. It has become an enterprise that is too unwieldy in an age when corporations must be nimble and efficient, many experts believe."

So make sure your choices are well thought out and that you have organizational skills and leadership to manage them successfully.

You can't be afraid to fail. However, when you are in the process of prioritizing strategies, an important question to ask is, "What can I afford to lose?" I have invested in a couple of Broadway shows. Of course, I looked at the prospectus with the projected financials, but just as with any new venture, you may as well put your finger up to the wind. As their name implies, they are nothing more than projections. My point is that when I invest, I look at it from the perspective of how much I can afford to lose, not how much I think I can make on that investment.

My most recent Broadway investment was *Fun Home*. I had been approached to invest in other shows, but I chose *Fun Home*, based not on the prospectus (although it looked solid) but because the storyline was about a girl who grew up in a funeral home. My parents owned a funeral home, so it seemed meant to be. As it turned out, I made a smart decision. The show won five Tony Awards including Best Musical. Sometimes intuition is stronger than all the projections and research in the world.

As a business leader, you need to consider new opportunities without a myopic focus on the number. If you try a new product, hire a new person, or incorporate a new process, ask yourself what is a reasonable amount you can invest that won't sink your business or division if it doesn't work out. And that cost should be viewed not only in terms of dollars but also in relationship to the drain on your team and the risk to your brand.

According to the HP Memory Project, Bill Hewlett ordered a market research report that suggested there would be no market for a handheld scientific electronic calculator. In 1972, the cost for one of the new gadgets would have been almost double the price of standard calculators that were on the market at the time. Therefore, the report forecast that the company wouldn't sell more than 1,000 a month. Hewlett made a bold decision to move forward by manufacturing 1,000 of the HP 35. Sales went through the roof, exceeding 10,000 per month.

In Chapter 8, "The Financial Edge," I'll explain the importance of listening to the story your company's numbers are telling you. However, when you're exploring new opportunities to create the One-Percent Edge, you shouldn't look at them in a vacuum. My doctor is incredible. Every year when I go for my physical, he reviews all my medical lab results with me, but then he talks to me about how I'm feeling. He once explained that numbers are just part of the process; he has to listen to the patient to get a complete picture. When weighing whether to make an investment, consider your projections, but listen to your market, your team, your investors, and most important, your gut. After all, as the leader, you'll be responsible for executing the strategy.

Cut the Dead Weight: No Sacred Cows

"Every organization must be prepared to abandon everything it does to survive the future."

—PETER DRUCKER

As you prioritize, be prepared to cut the dead weight. Start with your products or services. Are you losing market share? Has your profit margin been squeezed? Are your competitors doing well when you're struggling? Does it seem that your product or service is always "on sale"? Is your team comprised of the right people? Are you leveraging the right resources for productivity and profitability? Is the size of your market shrinking? Is the relevance of your product or service diminishing?

When you strive to continually innovate your business, you need to question every aspect of it, not just the product/service offering. All businesses have a limited amount of bandwidth. So if there is an element of your company that's bogging you down, now is time to cut the cord. Let the old make way for the new.

In the introduction, I shared the story of the demise of the Firestone tire company. In the late 1960s, many viewed it as one of the best-managed companies in the nation. However, its great success may have been a principle reason why it failed to respond appropriately when the radial tire was introduced to the domestic market. As the company faced new competition from abroad, it clung to its old ways of operating. Instead of reengineering its production processes for radial tires' higher quality standards, it simply tweaked them.

Additionally, Firestone failed to close many of its plants that produced the old type of tires, even though it was clear that there would soon be virtually no market for them. By 1979, the company had to rent warehouses to store unsold merchandise. That year, its domestic tire business burned through $200 million in cash. Eventually, the company was sold to Bridgestone at a fraction of the price it would have commanded a decade earlier.

The sale to Bridgestone is telling. While Firestone was content with being considered one of the best-managed U.S. firms in the 1960s, Bridgestone (a Japanese company) was busy adopting innovative quality control systems that had been developed by American engineers, most notably W. Edwards Deming.

We talk about market disruption today that is fueled or made possible by technology, but disruption is nothing new. In the 1970s, the Japanese quality control revolution began to cause just as much disruption, if not more. U.S. automakers were relegated to second-tier status (we examine this more in Chapter 7, "The Process Edge"), and the exodus of consumer-electronics manufacturers went into overdrive.

Related to the topic of quality, I want to share some important advice: As you work to improve the quality of your product or service, there will be times when you are analyzing the cost of a given improvement measured against the savings you will experience in efficiency, such as less waste and more time on task. You will be tempted to find the place where you think you are getting the maximum return on your investment.

I suggest that you spend a bit more to push your quality higher than your data suggest. Investing more heavily in quality improvement will pay you back in increased goodwill with your customers and clients. Providing an unquestionably better product or service will make your business stand out in a crowded market.

Aside from boosting loyalty, this sends a positive message to your employees, and in many cases, it makes their jobs easier.

As you follow the One-Percent Edge process, remember not to let emotions about your product, service, process, or people skew your objectivity. When the writing is on the wall, read it and pay attention. Don't rest on your laurels, don't grieve over transformations, and never base today's feelings of self-worth on yesterday's accomplishments.

Step 3: Create Your Action Plan

Start by listing your strategies and your assumptions about them. By articulating the assumptions, you'll be in a position to judge whether they prove true down the road. Then, put together a timeline, goals, and objectives and make sure that everyone in your organization understands their individual roles and accountabilities. It's important to revisit this. Too many action plans are forgotten just as quickly as they were created. Remember, we're talking about a way of doing business that changes your company's DNA; that kind of change doesn't "take" without constant reinforcement.

It's also smart to include your analysis of risk factors. What you can afford to lose? What happens if it fails? What competitive risks are on the horizon? Did you choose the correct infrastructure?

This is not your grandfather's five-year plan, by the way. This plan is designed to propel you forward quickly. In today's market, time is of the essence. Agility is key, and rigid five-year plans won't give you the flexibility you need to adapt to market changes.

"You have to give up the pretense that you can predict the future," explains Lowell Bryan, a director at McKinsey & Company. Bryan said leaders need to "navigate" their way through this more-dynamic era. Gone are the days of when your budgeting process could essentially assume economic certainty. "How can you say today what the economy will be like even six months from now?" he asked. Just-in-time decision making is a requirement today, Bryan contends.[4]

Step 4: **Execute**

No plan is good without action. Once you've decided on your direction, get going. Don't get paralyzed with perfection. You can tweak and tinker with it as you move forward, learning as you go what works and what doesn't. Waiting too long to perfect everything may result in losing your window of opportunity. Someone else who is more agile will sweep in and seize the moment.

Step 5: **Measure and Review**

Innovative leaders need to be resilient and be willing to walk away from failed strategies. An idea may have seemed like the greatest thing since sliced bread, but now you find you can't dig your heels in and throw good money after bad. And, I might add, timing is of the essence. Clinging to a failing strategy is futile, and it prevents you from moving on to better opportunities.

Pixar Director Andrew Stanton said, "People need to be wrong as fast as they can. In a battle, if you're faced with two hills and you're unsure which one to attack, the right course of action is to hurry up and choose. If you find out it's the wrong hill, turn around and attack the other one."[5]

Stay the Course or Adjust

After reviewing your results, your team and you must make the decision to stay the course, make adjustments, or abandon the initiative completely. That's why making initial assumptions and establishing measurements and benchmarks is important. At this point in the process, if a decision is made to abandon the strategy, do it quickly and move forward. Learn from your mistakes and keep the momentum going forward. Breakthrough growth requires a tolerance for experimentation and a departure from past playbooks.

Some of the biggest brands today have had failures and flops. In 1993, Apple launched the Newton personal digital assistant, which was too bulky and expensive. HP founders Bill Hewlett and Dave Packard introduced a bowling alley foul-line indicator, a clock drive for a telescope, and a shock machine designed to help people lose weight before they arrived at the products we know as HP today. Procter & Gamble (P&G) was a candle maker in Cincinnati.

Step 6: **Repeat**

Because achieving the One-Percent Edge is a process—a mode of operating your business—you must constantly repeat the strategy from the beginning. By implementing this process you'll be better equipped to position your business to remain relevant despite changing market trends.

CHAPTER 2

The Leadership Edge

"Leadership is the capacity to translate vision into reality."

—**WARREN BENNIS**

N ow that you've seen how the six-step process works, it's up to you to take the reins and lead your organization with this approach to changing times. For most of you, adopting this process will require a major shift in your mindset. Remember: Change your attitude, change your results.

- ▶ Are company leaders walking the walk or just talking the talk?
- ▶ Do they have the right tools and resources to work smarter and make effective decisions?
- ▶ Do they think about, talk about, and commit to enhancing the customer experience?
- ▶ Are they looking beyond the horizon for new opportunities and unmet needs?
- ▶ Have they articulated a strong vision that resonates with employees, customers, partners, and vendors?
- ▶ How do our leaders empower their teams?
- ▶ Is senior management open to change?

The idea of change is scary. There is an element of the fear of the unknown. The One-Percent Edge process is a disciplined approach to innovation, a focused, incremental development of your business at every level that allows your business to be proactive rather than reactive. And as we've discussed, reactive strategies frequently don't work.

Rah-Rah! So What? Walk the Talk

When I worked in the corporate world, I wrote speeches for the CEO. Once a year he would give his pep talk to the entire company. In those days before streaming video, the event occurred live at our headquarters; we'd tape it and mail it to all our offices around the country so they could host gatherings in their locations. By the time I left the company, I could practically write the speech in my sleep. There was a great deal of rah-rah, with enthusiastic goals to be "second to none." Several times I even produced snazzy videos to go along with his remarks.

These were fun events, but despite claims of innovative strategies and accolades for the entire team, within a week or so it was back to business as usual—the same old same old. In fact, the year after I left the company, they held the event at a fancy hotel and flew in many executives and managers from the United States as well as Europe to attend. Each person received a very nice and expensive gift. The very next week they laid off hundreds of people. Some of my former associates said the employees would rather have saved a few jobs with all the money that was spent on the "rah-rah" event.

Motivational events can be inspiring, and it is a good way to get your team geared up for your big vision. However, as we know, actions speak louder than words. When all the words have been spoken and the soiree is a memory, inaction will lose momentum and result in a team of disengaged employees.

As a marketing executive in the corporate world in financial services, I worked with bean counters to justify nearly every spend. Today, when I attend these types of conferences as a speaker, I will sometimes look around, think about all the money being spent, and wonder how the company measures its return on investment.

So whether you're spending time and talent, or actual dollars, or "all of the above," you must have a plan of execution. The follow-up, measurements, and adjustments of the One-Percent Edge process will provide your team with ways to witness the success and be part of it.

Taking Action: Building Skills to Lead with the Edge

First and foremost, to leverage the One-Percent Edge, a leader must be willing to let go of preconceived ideas regarding just about everything. Your psychological perspectives are often the chains that bind your hands. There is no textbook, no MBA class, and no seminar or business guide that can provide a step-by-step process toward growth. In fact, I once taught an MBA course on growth strategies for entrepreneurs where I stressed the importance of recognizing that when you're studying a strategy it's already obsolete. The only thing constant in the business world today is change, and change is happening at an ever-quickening pace. If you're mired in the status quo, the chances of remaining relevant diminish. So as you begin this journey, clear the cobwebs out of your head and get ready for an exciting new adventure.

Be Open-Minded

All of us who lead businesses usually feel confident in our ideas. But to fully leverage the One-Percent Edge, you can't hold on tightly to your ideas. If you come up with a strategy you feel is just what the business needs, it's easy to become attached to it. Let's face it: We all have egos. However, in order to get the business moving forward, it's imperative that you listen to feedback from all your company's stakeholders. A failure to listen can result in significant missteps and even business failures.

The best leaders refuse to surround themselves with people who will merely massage their egos and agree with everything they say or suggest. Writing for the *Harvard Business Review*, William C. Taylor, cofounder of *Fast Company*, claimed that true leaders have a sense of humility and invite dissent. According to Taylor, "humility in the service of ambition is the most effective and sustainable mindset for leaders who aspire to do big things in a world filled with huge unknowns."[1]

Make Real-Time Decisions Quickly

Today, business leaders can make well-informed decisions based on real-time data. It's key to use this information to review results of the strategies you're employing to create the One-Percent Edge. In the chapter on process, I'll show you tools that you can use to build real agility into your business assessments. Your numbers are telling you an important story. You need to listen carefully. That means you must not try to rationalize the results. Try to look at the data as objectively as you can. Trust your numbers.

Make Bold Decisions with Reason

Nothing is worse than a leader who is constantly changing her position. As they say, pick a lane and stay in it until it's obvious it's a dead end. The One-Percent Edge process provides a mechanism to evaluate opportunities, determine which are the smartest choices at the time, create a plan of action, and then evaluate the results. Your team needs to know that the process works and that once a commitment is made to a strategy, everyone needs to give it their all.

You may have worked with leaders who manage by the flavor-of-the-month approach. There is always something new, and yet there is no real clarification for the change. As I said earlier, change for change's sake isn't a strategy. So once a decision is reached, you need to be able to explain how and why it was made. When you review results, that's the time to consider adjustments or a complete change of course.

Never be quick to judge.

"Oh that will never work."

"Are you kidding? What a crazy idea."

If I had a dime for every time I heard someone say, "Susan, you don't understand, my business is different. That would never work in my business," I'd be a very rich woman. Those phrases are not part of the vocabulary of a leader using the One-Percent Edge process. You must foster an environment where your team members feel safe to push the envelope. One of my bosses used to tell me he was giving me enough room to fail. In order words, he wanted me to be responsible and accountable for developing new ideas and opportunities.

Of course, you need to celebrate your team's successes. You know how parents mark their children's height on the wall so they can actually see the advancement they've made? Visuals can help your team as well. How can you illustrate what your business will look like with new strategies? When you meet or exceed your goals ring the bells, blow the whistles, and shout it out!

However, it's okay to break things as you focus on achieving the One-Percent Edge. Some companies even go as far as to reward flops. Why? Because it shows initiative and the desire to try new things. Procter & Gamble has a Dare to Try award. The gaming company Supercell is known to break open a bottle of champagne when a game fails. For a good laugh, check out Ben & Jerry's graveyard of flavors. Yes, even Ben & Jerry's can step in it sometimes. Imagine eating ice cream called Schweddy Balls!

While your business might not have significant resources to test new strategies, the same general concept can be applied by testing a new innovation with a small group before rolling it out company-wide. Quite frankly, if you're leading a smaller organization, you have a better opportunity to leverage the One-Percent Edge process because you can implement a plan quickly and adjust quickly as well. However, as your organization grows—and it will, if you stick with this process—be sure to foster that entrepreneurial spark so that the business doesn't become a slow-moving elephant.

Integrity and Authenticity

A lot has been written about leadership, but becoming a leader in the One-Percent Edge environment isn't an academic study. It's an exercise of common sense. Change is always scary in any aspect of your life. So as a business leader, you need to make sure people have confidence in you, and by confidence I mean trust.

Myriad research studies show what people want most in leaders is honesty and integrity. Garnering that kind of trust as a leader is simple. Always be open and honest; keep your messages simple and built on a foundation of your company's mission and values. You need a diversity of ideas and experiences to help your company build the One-Percent Edge. You also need to win your team's hearts. You want them invested in the vision.

In innovative organizations, a natural tension may arise: the need for diversity in order to generate creative ideas for success in an increasingly heterogeneous market environment and the requirement to create unity of purpose so everyone can be rowing in the same direction.

This creates a major challenge for leadership. While you must make and enforce internal rules that require mutual respect up and down your organizational ranks, these qualities need to be modeled. Work to put together a leadership team that reflects the kind of diversity you want for your business. Respect divergent points of views and ideas.

Be open and honest with your team. When your employees begin to sense that there is someone else behind the curtain, they may continue to perform, but they won't be fully engaged, and morale will drop along with productivity and profitability.

If you treat people with respect and create an atmosphere where even a seemingly off-the-wall idea gets fair consideration, it goes a long way toward creating unity. And more importantly perhaps, it goes a long way toward achieving success, and in business, success is the great unifier—everyone wants to get on board.

Appreciate the Importance of Emotional Intelligence

We often talk about "the smartest person in the room." We appreciate intelligence, and since we know that it's a respected attribute, if we think we have it, we tend to show it off.

But, when you're leading people, being the smartest person in the room isn't enough, and it might not even be one of the most important qualities. Having emotional intelligence—commonly referred to as EQ (for emotional quotient)—is critical for leaders.

People with EQ can recognize, identify, and manage their own emotions as well as the emotions of those they are engaging with. Leaders can't allow their emotions to run away with them. The first step is being able to recognize the point in which your emotions start wanting to call the shots and then being able to rein them in.

You might object. You might say that you can't control the emotions of others, which is true to an extent. However, I'm sure you know people who have a natural calming effect during tense, emotional situations as well as people with the ability to cheer others up. There are people I want to be around when I'm starting to feel a little down.

A friend of mine was once the adult supervisor at a school event for high school juniors and seniors. A few of the kids managed to sneak out of the restaurant where it was being held. They were rounded up quickly, but a mom of one of the sneaky kids was extremely irate, and she let loose on my friend.

My friend listened and repeated a few of her points to make sure he understood. After her rant was over, the mom said, "I'm not mad anymore." She understood that her son hadn't really done anything wrong, and she was surprised that her anger had dissipated so quickly. Having realized that the mom wasn't angry with him, my high-EQ friend didn't take her rant personally.

To put it simply, leaders with high EQ make situations better almost by their mere presence.

Looking in the Mirror

As you continue your journey to understand, adopt, and implement the One-Percent Edge process, you'll see that the guidance covers virtually every aspect of your company. No matter the size of your organization, the question then becomes, Do you have the knowledge and experience to implement the process in such divergent business areas?

The best leaders know what they don't know, and they bring the right people onto their teams to provide the leadership in the areas where they are not the best suited to lead.

In the early days of the Internet, an acquaintance of mine was working at a company that was transitioning from being a catalog bookseller to an Internet bookseller. The founder had a strong background in finance and a lot of experience in the mail order catalog business. He was, however, fairly computer illiterate.

At first, he insisted on making too many decisions regarding the company's Internet strategy, but fortunately he soon realized that he was in over his head on much of that part of the operation. So he handed over the technical and Internet marketing side of the company to people with more understanding and concentrated on the finances and backend fulfillment operation, which were his strengths.

What are your strengths? Your weaknesses? Like the old adage says, a team is only as strong as its weakest player. As you internalize what needs to be done to apply the One-Percent Edge process to your business, ask yourself, Are you the right person to lead in each area? You can certainly give direction and inspire others who are working in areas that aren't exactly your strong suit, but you don't want to hamper them.

Before we end this little look in the mirror, take a quick inventory of the following attributes that tend to make a good leader. Many of these may be part of your natural personality. When individuals possess a large measure of all or most of these, we give them the label "natural born leader." (However, I think most of us would admit that we're lacking in a few areas, which is not a big problem, because in most cases we can improve in those areas if we are willing to try).

Take a few minutes to reflect on these qualities of a good business leader:

- Demonstrates a consistent attitude and actions
- Follows through on commitments
- Is loyal to others
- Is readily available
- Gives praise
- Plans
- Accepts responsibility for business decisions
- Delegates well
- Knows the difference between the important issues and small details
- Is a good listener and communicator
- Treats people fairly and honestly
- Is an idea/vision person
- Is the person people turn to for advice
- Isn't afraid to get advice from others

- Enjoys new projects
- Possesses a high EQ

No Overnight Successes

How long will it take to build the One-Percent process into your company's modus operandi? It depends on you, the business leader. Your ability to communicate, commit, and lead the execution will determine the length of time it takes to get your team on board. It could happen immediately, it might take a week, a month, or even longer. However, the longer it takes, the less likely you will be able to position your company—your brand—as a business with the edge. The most relevant companies are those that are in sync with the market.

With the One-Percent Edge process, there's no end to the story. It's a methodology that requires constant reevaluation and agility.

CHAPTER 3

The Customer Edge

"Good is the enemy of great."

—JIM COLLINS

D igital technology and information—including big data—have changed the relationships between businesses and customers in ways that were almost unimaginable a generation ago. Your potential customers and clients know more about your business than ever before, and you have the potential to know more about them. Both sides have more power to pick and choose whom they do business with and how that business is conducted.

The challenge for business leaders is to see this relationship from both sides: You need to understand how prospects discover, view, and interact with your brand, and at the same time you have to find the group of consumers that are the most likely to respond to your brand's competitive edge. Once this group is identified, you must communicate with them and care for them properly.

- Are we giving customers a reason to change their buying habits and fall in love with us?
- Are we using technology, tools, and resources to best serve our customers?
- Do we constantly enhance the customer experience and deliver on expectations?
- Have we articulated a strong vision to our customer base and our prospects?
- Are our teams trained and empowered to serve the customers?
- Are we responsive to market shifts and changes in customer buying habits?

Here's the deal: No matter what industry or business you're in, you're in the people business. And the balance of power has shifted. Customers have the power today. Whether you're business to business (B2B) or business to consumer (B2C), customers know more about your business, product, and service than ever. They research and comparison shop before they make buying decisions. They read online reviews and ratings.

In a survey of 1,200 U.S. consumers, [24]7, the global leader in customer-engagement solutions, found that four in five consumers (79 percent) will take their business elsewhere within a week of experiencing poor customer service.

The Risks for Business Leaders

Companies of all sizes miss the mark when it comes to understanding the growing power of the customer. According to PV Kannan, founder and CEO of [24]7, consumers have more options than ever, so they don't feel compelled to stay loyal to a given company when the customer experience falls short.

"The way customers engage with brands has dramatically shifted, yet many enterprises' approach to customer service and sales is stuck in yesterday's paradigm," said Kannan. "For this reason, it's more important than ever for brands to be where their customers are, and allow them to engage on their own terms."[1]

Talking about being a customer-centric company doesn't make it so. Your plan must have the commitment of top leadership. You must establish metrics to measure the customer experience just as you would for any other aspect of your business.

To ensure you're getting accurate results, start with a benchmark: Survey your customers about their experiences. Establish a customer advisory panel to get a sense of where you stand currently. Another telling exercise is to ask your customers to describe your business with one word. Then make those words into an abstract visual with the least used being in small print and the most mentioned in much larger fonts. Is this the way you want your company to be seen? Is it the way you thought your customers viewed you?

As part of your prioritization process, choose the areas that are most problematic first. What steps can you take to change the customer experience? What steps should be taken to reinforce areas where your business is strong?

Don't forget to get a read on your employees' satisfaction. It's a fundamental truth that happy employees lead to happy customers. All the people in your organization need to recognize the importance of the customer experience and how they are responsible for the achievement. And you must emphasize that the people you serve are the reason you're in business. Customers are the ultimate bosses. Customers pay your salaries.

Because the most difficult part of the One-Percent Edge process is execution, appoint one or more internal champion (depending on the breadth of your organization). Incentivize team members who exemplify the spirit of a customer-centric organization.

Examine Customer Retention

One number critically important to focus on when evaluating your success with customers is the lifetime value (LTV) of a customer. Are you retaining customers or are they moving in and out as if they were in a revolving door? The simplest formula for how to work out LTV is to multiply three numbers: the value (net profit) of each sale to a customer, the number of sales made to a customer in a year, and the number of years a customer remains a customer (if a customer drops out sooner than one year, this would be a fraction).

For example, if you net $100 for each sale to a customer who makes 12 purchases in a year, and you retain the customer for 10 years, that customer's lifetime value is $100 x 12 x 10 = $12,000.

Is your company focused on customer retention? Many organizations put a greater emphasis on acquiring new business than retaining existing customers. As a result, existing customers may feel ignored and unappreciated. They hold the perception that once the company has customers on board, it doesn't need to pay close attention anymore. So those customers may start looking elsewhere. If there is a sense of complacency within your organization, you need to wake up your team and develop strategies that will turn your existing customers into raving fans.

Cut the Dead Weight

Not all customers are created equal. Not all customers should be treated equally. To maintain your innovative, growth focus, you need to cut the dead weight by eliminating certain customers at times or streamlining the service level.

Not long ago, I published a guest post from the noted customer service guru Shep Hyken titled "Don't Just Fix the Problem. Fix the Customer."[2] I thought that was an interesting headline because aren't customers always supposed to be right? Shep wisely points out that it's just as important to repair your relationship with customers as it is to deal with the technical side of whatever problems they are experiencing with your product or service. However, there are times when you need to sever your relationship with certain customers or clients; as much as we hate to do it, sometimes we have to fire the customer.

This is, of course, a decision that cannot be taken lightly. Right now you may be feeling uneasy about one or more of your customers, but you just aren't comfortable about what to do next. Let me give you some perspective, guidelines, and rationale that will help you make the right decision and give you the confidence to carry out your decision.

The Demanding Customer

You know the costs that go into manufacturing your product, buying your inventory, or providing your service. However, do you know the hours your team spends selling and servicing these items? (In Chapter 7, "The Process Edge," I'll go into more depth about time tracking.)

If you own a print shop, for example, and you find that one customer takes up three times as many hours as your average customer, it's probably time to start turning down that person's business. The same thing applies to your sales force: If closing a sale and maintaining a particular account eats up far more time than the average account, you may be best served by moving on.

It's true that time is money. And when certain customers routinely take far more time than average, you have entered into a lost-opportunity situation; your time would be better spent finding new and less-demanding customers.

The Disruptive Customer

Some customers are a pain in the you-know-what to deal with. If they are merely picky or eccentric, that's usually fine. However, there are some behaviors that cross the line, such as:

- Disrespecting your employees
- Ignoring personal boundaries
- Dishonesty
- Causing too much negativity

You need to put your team first. If your employees feel safe and happy at work, that will be reflected in everything they do, and your small business will benefit greatly. If they feel threatened, belittled, or engulfed in a cloud of negativity, that too will be reflected in their work. Productivity will go down. Customer relationships will suffer, and turnover will go through the roof.

Also, if a customer proves to be dishonest, it's impossible to develop a long-term business relationship. You should feel confident that your customers will keep up their end of the agreement. If you continue to work with a customer who you know is dishonest, you will eventually get burned—and it will be your fault.

In the long run, your business will prosper more without these problem customers.

The Late-Paying Customer

While it's common for businesses of all sizes to have to deal with late-paying customers, it is more challenging for a smaller organization. There must be a point at which you draw the line, stop extending credit, and cease selling to or servicing the customer.

Look at the progress the customer is making on what she owes you. Is it significantly dropping, staying about the same, or even increasing? If the customer isn't showing a commitment to paying down the balance, it's time to break the relationship, send the bill to collections, and move on.

The Needy Customer

When I described customers who may be picky or a bit eccentric I was referring to the person-to-person level. Now I want to talk about customers who are always demanding special treatment or changes to your product or service that no one else ever seems to need. I'm talking about the high-maintenance customer.

If the changes or tweaks are minor, there is no reason to let them upset you (they might even be clues for business enhancements). However, if they are more significant and constant and reduce your profit margins, you need to take action. These may also be the customers who are always asking for special deals and seem offended if you balk at their requests.

The One-Percent Edge comes from retaining the right customers—those who will bring in the most revenue over time. So show your problem customers the door.

Staying Relevant to Your Customers

Do you have friends whose appearance hasn't changed since high school? Ask for a headshot and you may get something that looks like it might have been a senior picture. As part of the baby boomer generation, I've done my best to evolve with the times. (Some even say I don't look my age.) My peers often look stodgy and dated even though the opposite could be true. We all know people judge a book by its cover.

The same is true for businesses. If your company has looked and felt the same for decades, you may be turning off the newcomers. For example, Cadillac, the well-known luxury car brand, began slipping in popularity because younger buyers viewed Cadillacs as something their grandparents drove. The average age of a luxury car buyer, 61.

According to the U.S. Census Bureau, the nation's 75.4 million millennials (ages 18–24) have surpassed its 74.9 million baby boomers (ages 51–69) and are now the nation's largest living generation. Additionally, generation X (ages 35–50) is projected to pass the boomers in population by 2028. So companies are being forced to refresh and rethink their branding and product positioning to remain relevant.

In response to the shifting demographic to younger car buyers, Cadillac is working to appeal to this market by offering redesigned, sleeker models with impressive infotainment packages. It even unveiled a new logo. The laurel surrounding the Cadillac crest is now history. The new crest is "sleeker and streamlined," designed to best represent the brand's long-running art-and-science design philosophy, according to the website MotorAuthority. But so far the data shows that the ship will be slow to turn.

"Once you get labeled as [a brand] associated with the older buyer, you're really in a bind with younger buyers," said Karl Brauer, senior director of insights at vehicle information provider Kelley Blue Book. He added, "No manufacturer wants to be known as the old persons' car brand."[3]

Another brand that is recognizing the need to reposition itself to attract a younger audience is Nordstrom. Founded in 1901, the upscale retailer tends to skew toward an older demographic with discretionary income. But it recognizes that in order to attract the new kids in town and maintain relevancy, it must shift its positioning. The company has updated its look and added a store within a store called Space focused on young designers and trendier styles.

It has also turned to social media platforms such as Snapchat and Instagram, popular with a younger audience, to engage this target market. Additionally, the introduction of the company's outlet store, Nordstrom Rack, is providing exposure to a completely different audience. There is only about 10-to-20 percent overlap in customers who shop in the retail store and the outlet. "Everyone in our line of business needs new customers," said Nordstrom spokesperson Pamela Lopez.

Are You Ready for These Demographic Facts?

Diversity is a term that gets bandied about in a wide variety of settings. It's used so much and so often that it's in danger of losing its meaning. Or perhaps we're in danger of failing to appreciate its significance.

I just mentioned some important attributes of millennials, but the picture is much more complicated—diverse—than that. I don't think I'm overstating the case when I say that the consumer base today is divided into more groups and subgroups than ever before.

As a nation of immigrants, the United States has long been the most diverse large country on the planet, and in fact its diversity has grown in recent decades for two basic reasons:

- People are living longer than ever.
- People are moving to the United States in bigger numbers and from a wider variety of nations than ever.

To expand on that first point, baby boomers, generation Xers, millennials (generation Y), and generation Z are all significant buying groups. We even have members of the silent generation—those born during World War II and before—among us.

The situation gets even more interesting when you overlay the second point on these generations: The older generations are somewhat more homogenous, but as you work your way down to the younger generations, the diversity becomes more striking.

When the Brookings Institution examined 2015 census data, it concluded that the millennial generation is playing a pivotal role in turning the United States into a "majority minority" nation. According to Brookings, 75 percent of the U.S. population 55 and older is white. That number falls to less than 56 percent among the millennials and just 51.5 percent of generation Z. By the year 2044, demographers predict that minority groups will make up more than 50 percent of the population.[4]

If your business depends on a local group of consumers, these percentages fluctuate widely. Minorities already make up more than 50 percent of the millennial cohort in 10 states: California, Texas, Arizona, Florida, Georgia, New Jersey, Nevada, New Mexico, Hawaii, and Maryland.

If you're doing business in one of those states, that doesn't come as any news to you. However, if your state isn't on that list, pay attention anyway because they are leading the way. Many other states, including New York, Illinois, Virginia, North Carolina, and

South Carolina are just a few percentage points behind. Business owners who depend on local trade would be wise to study what's working in the states that are on the leading edge of this diversity wave and use those successes as models for their businesses going forward.

Let me say one thing about generation Z that, I believe, hits a lot of the touch points important for relating to prospects today. *USA Today* ran a story describing Target's efforts to market to generation Z. It created a new clothing brand, Art Class, to appeal to that demographic. And, as part of its marketing efforts, Target has enlisted the help of social media influencer Mercer Henderson.

Mercer's age? 14.

Finding the Silver Lining

This demographic shift creates the classic challenge-versus-opportunity environment for your business. Reaching these diverse groups of buyers is a tall order, but at the same time you can view each of these segments as a possible niche market. If you're trying to be all things to all people, you may have set yourself an impossible goal. But if you shape your product or service to be the ideal fit for any of these groups, you can build a successful business. Further, if small changes in your product, service, and/or marketing allow you to dial in other groups, you have the power to exploit several niche markets with little additional cost or effort.

The Fox Entertainment Group has made one of the most specifically targeted plays in this area with Fox Deportes (formerly Fox Sports en Español). The media company also founded a Spanish-language cable news network, MundoFox, for a more general Spanish-speaking audience. Apparently, that venture didn't hold very much promise, so it was sold and eventually died a quiet death.[5]

By defining a narrower niche—sports fans who prefer Spanish-language broadcasts—Fox has a much better chance to engage its ideal prospects and establish the kind of long-term relationships that lead to a profitable network. With the sports channel, it's easier for Fox to discover which sports and events hit the sweet spot with its audience.

Case Study: When a Luxury Brand Provides Bargain-Basement Customer Service

Imagine writing a check to a luxury brand to pay for a purchase in full and two months later the company hadn't applied the funds and your credit report is about to get dinged. That is what happened to me with a major automobile dealer.

For the first year that I owned a second home in Florida, I rented a car each time I visited. I thought about buying a car to keep in Florida, but I'm not keen on car shopping. So when a friend casually mentioned that she didn't like the luxury car she'd leased two months earlier, I asked if I could take over the three-year lease, which would free her up to find something she liked better. That was in August.

The carmaker sent us the necessary transfer forms, and I wrote a check in full to pay the entire lease starting with the August payment. However, an August and September payment was also deducted from my friend's account.

Usher in the month of September, and customer service had not advised us of the status of the transfer. Eventually, I was notified that the transfer was complete. A review of my checking account confirmed that the carmaker had cashed my check.

I called customer service to find out how they would reconcile two additional payments. After spending at least thirty minutes on the phone, I was told that accounting would review it and would probably refund the excess.

Then at the end of October, much to my displeasure, I received a bill to make a monthly payment. So I placed yet another call to customer service. This time the representative said they had indeed cashed my check for the full amount of the lease term, but they needed my permission to apply the funds. Seriously? Why didn't anyone call me or send me a letter explaining that additional step?

When I tweeted about my experience, the company's response was slow and placating at best. The irony of the situation was that they told me to call customer service.

While I like my new car, I'll never deal with the company again. My friends and business associates all agree that you should expect more from such a luxury brand. Wrapped up in this experience are some good lessons for your business:

Be ready for exceptions. Not every customer has the same needs. While most customers pay their lease agreements month by month, I preferred to pay in advance. This threw their system for a loop. From my point of view, they should have been happy to receive their money in advance and have thanked me for it; instead, they gave me a headache.

Train customer service personnel for complex situations. The scenario I described is not uncommon. By the time a customer decides to reach out to a front-line employee, the situation is already complex. Meanwhile, the landscape has changed dramatically, leaving way for frantic outcries from disgruntled customers on social media platforms.

Give employees the authority they need. I suspect that somewhere in this drama my situation required customer service employees to take actions they don't normally take. Trust, train, and empower your team members sufficiently so you can unleash them to solve problems on the spot.

Respond in real time. For better or for worse, the Internet and social-media-based customer service have made consumers expect immediate responses to their issues. The luxury carmaker I dealt with is a legacy company, but it needs to be just as social media savvy as an eager start-up staffed by millennials. As Babe Ruth once said, "Yesterday's home runs don't win today's games."

Offer more than a great product. There is no arguing the fact that this manufacturer makes wonderful cars. However, the consumer relationship goes deeper than the product; it extends to the company, and especially the parts of the company that interact with the consumer. Today we talk about the customer experience. If that experience falls short of the mark, your business will suffer, no matter how great your product is.

Admit and correct mistakes quickly. If you do make a mistake—it happens—be accountable and be quick to rectify the situation.

Learn from companies that get it right. When it comes to developing your One-Percent Edge, being good is just the beginning. Being exceptional must be your goal. You need to develop strategies to go beyond good. After all, good merely satisfies customers, whereas exceptional delights them. A satisfied customer can easily be lost to a competitor, but a delighted customer is yours for life.

Nordstrom is a company that gets it. The retailer offers unconditional guarantees, and it gives employees the authority to manage that expectation. You may have heard the legend that captures Nordstrom's customer service ethic: A man walked into the Nordstrom department store in Fairbanks, Alaska, with two snow tires. He proceeded to the customer service counter, put the tires down, and asked for his money back. The clerk saw the price on the side of the tires, reached into the cash register, and handed the man $145—even though Nordstrom doesn't sell tires. Now there's a company that knows how to deliver a *wow* customer experience.

When it comes to anything involving speed and measuring who is the fastest, nobody remembers who took second place.

Jesse Owens's win in the 200-meter dash at the 1936 Summer Olympic Games in Berlin will always be remembered. We're still making movies about it. But who remembers Matthew Robinson, who broke the old Olympic record on his way to winning the silver medal? Although Robinson was quite an accomplished athlete, he was overshadowed first by Owens and later by his younger brother, a Hall of Fame baseball player whose first name was Jackie and wore the number 42. Hey, they're still making movies about him, too.

Customers won't give you many chances to get it right. With vendors so easily accessible via the Internet, jumping your ship to sample the ride on your competitor's boat takes no more effort than a few mouse clicks. Further, when customers engage your customer service system, they will always be measuring it against all the other customer service experiences they have had. They'll be drawing up a little mental report card and giving you scores on topics such as:

- Were you faster or slower than customer service at other businesses they frequent?
- Were your employees friendly?
- Did your employees have the knowledge, ability, and authority to solve their problems?
- Did the problem get solved on the first contact with customer service?

Make sure it's your company standing on the podium for the gold medal of customer service.

Using Social Media for Customer Service: Connect the Dots

Harvard Business Review ran an article with the headline "Your Company Should Be Helping Customers on Social" (July 2015). I think that sums up the bottom line very well: You should be offering great customer service with social media. According to the J.D. Power and Associates 2013 *Social Media Benchmark Study*, 67 percent of customers have used a company's social media channels for customer service related issues, and they expect a quick response.[6] Among respondents to the study who have ever attempted to contact a brand, product, or company through social media for customer support, 32 percent expect a response time within 30 minutes, and 42 percent expect a 60-minute response time. Fifty-seven percent expect the same response time at night and on weekends as during normal business hours.[7]

There is no one-size-fits-all pattern for offering great customer service with social media. Companies need to understand how their customers use social media and then develop a strategy that addresses their usage patterns. The appropriate strategy, tools, and platforms change depending on the size and nature of your business. Twitter has been the platform of choice for companies large and small that want to offer great customer service with social media. With 140 characters, you can't explain how to change the water filter on a counter-depth, side-by-side refrigerator, but you can send a link to a page or PDF that provides complete instructions.

Because messages are short and to the point—and generally responded to quickly—consumers seem to prefer Twitter for a customer service pipeline. Major corporations devote separate accounts to serving customers, like Best Buy's @twelpforce.

When I related my poor experience with the luxury automaker, I noted how slow they were to respond with social media. When they finally did respond to my comments, they were of no help. All they sent was a standard line to placate me and appear as though they cared. Truthfully, that infuriated me more than if they hadn't responded at all.

Social media is an excellent tool to identify and address customer service issues in real time. However, the group that manages the social media likely doesn't have the authority to resolve the issue. So you get standard answers such as, "We're sorry you're having issues. Please contact our customer service department." If you persist with your comments, the social media manager will ask you to take it offline. After all, there's a massive audience listening to your complaint, and that can undo even the best marketing campaigns.

Nike created a separate Twitter account just for responding to customers' issues and concerns (@NikeSupport). Check out its Twitter feed and see how quickly it responds. A timely reply builds trust and confidence in the brand. Starbucks also has a separate Twitter account called @MyStarbucksIdea as an additional way to engage with customers. This account is a place where customers can submit and discuss ideas to make Starbucks better.[8]

Companies that get it right are reaping the rewards. People who use social media to get help are likely to spend more money with a company than those who don't use social media, said Jacqueline Anderson, director of product development for social media and text analytics at J.D. Power and Associates, speaking at the International Customer Service Association Annual Conference in 2013.

One final piece of advice on customer service and social media: If you have great employees, good products, and an excellent system, you won't find yourself cyberracing across the Internet trying to put out customer service fires. No matter what approach you take to providing social media customer service, if you're providing a great experience to begin with, your job will be much easier.

You're Being Measured Against the Highest Standards

I previously mentioned that with the easy availability of information over the Internet, it's likely that some of your prospects know as much about you as you do (or even more). Even if you aren't selling over the Internet, and even if you're a service provider, you need to know that because of the way commerce and information flow today, you're competing with the best companies in your sector. If you don't raise the customer service bar, someone else will; and even if you're not in direct competition with each other, your reputation will be tarnished.

Let me give you an example. A friend owns residential investment real estate in California. Several years ago, he moved to Tennessee and was recently looking to purchase investment property there. He did some online research and discovered that a city about two hours from his home is one of the better places in the country to buy investment property.

Investigating further, he began looking for potential property management companies. Because he would be buying property in a city more than a hundred miles away, he couldn't manage it himself.

As he researched property management firms, he found one that looked promising, so he dug a little deeper. He discovered that the firm had an Internet portal for property owners where they could get a real-time look at how their properties were performing: which tenants were current in rents, which were behind, who was being evicted, what kinds of repairs were being made, and more.

The property management company he had been using for many years in California offered nothing like that. Once a month he received several printed pages from the company that summarized income and expenses. While that was adequate, it didn't include any information on specific tenants or details on the exact nature of repairs. It was the bare minimum and delivered well after the month was over.

Although the property manager in California never knew it, a company located more than halfway across the nation had outshone him. When the time is convenient, my friend will find a better company. Meantime, I can guarantee you, now that he knows what good customer service looks like, he won't be recommending his old California property manager to anyone.

Let me give you another quick example that will apply to many businesses. Is your product or service social-media-sharing worthy? If you own a restaurant, are your entree portions big enough and well plated enough for their picture to be posted on social media? Your steak dinner will be judged against steak dinners from around the globe posted on Facebook and other social media platforms.

Virtually every business has the potential for a positive or negative social media mention. What you offer consumers will be measured against those companies that rate social media kudos—not to mention review sites like Yelp.

The lesson is that you can't narrowly focus on the competitor next door and feel secure if you think you have edged it out. Survey the best providers in your industry across the country, see what they are doing right, and implement it for yourself.

Little Things Matter

A company with the One-Percent Edge understands the importance of the small stuff. Sometimes it's the simple little things that can really set you apart and keep your customers coming back time and time again. Yet frequently the little things get overlooked.

As you evaluate your business, ask yourself: Would your customer describe the experience as delightful or amazing? What would you like your customer to say about your business?

It's the little things like remembering your customers' birthdays, saying congratulations for an accomplishment, keeping track of their buying preferences, or giving them a little lagniappe—a small gift given at the time of purchase. Little things, big results. It's the One-Percent difference. Here are a few of those "little things":

▶ **Smile.** A smile is contagious and makes people feel welcome. I've encountered so many bitter airline representatives who make you feel as though they are doing you a big favor when they are simply doing their jobs. When I encounter a gate agent or flight attendant who smiles at me and seems happy to help me, I thank them and send praise for them to the company. How do your team members rate? A simple smile is magnetic. Oh, and by the way, it takes fewer muscles to smile than it does to frown. Plus research from the 1970s and 1980s suggests that your facial expression might actually influence your mood. (Try putting a smile on your face and see if you feel happy.) So let your team know how important it is to smile when dealing with customers.

▶ **Do Whatever it Takes.** Everyone makes mistakes, and training your customer service team to quickly apologize for mistakes and rectify them is one of the most important "little things" you can do to enhance your customer service. Sometimes that means accepting responsibility for something that isn't your fault. Perception is reality. The goal is to do your best to satisfy your customer. My eye doctor is a perfect example of being accountable. I ordered a three-month supply of contact lenses, and after several weeks I hadn't received them. I called the office and they said their tracking information said the package was left by my front door, but they agreed to send another shipment. Shortly after I received the second shipment, my neighbor who had been out of town brought the first package over and explained it had been delivered to the wrong address. So I called the doctor's office and apologized and I asked them to charge me for the second shipment. They were appreciative because they would have been out several hundred dollars.

▶ **Use Common Sense.** One of the best ways to wow your customers is to go beyond what they're expecting. One of my favorite examples of building loyalty involves two competing discount shoe stores located next door to each other. I had reward coupons for both stores, but I didn't realize that the coupons had expired. The first store refused to accept the coupon even though it was only two days past the expiration date. It was the corporate policy. The second store gladly accepted my coupon, which turned out to be nearly a year old. Both coupons were only for $10 off, but the way the stores handled the situation spoke volumes. The first store lost a good customer over $10, because now I only shop at the second store.

▶ **Lagniappe.** Give your customer a little something extra. A lagniappe is "a small gift given a customer by a merchant at the time of a purchase" (such as a thirteenth doughnut on purchase of a dozen), or more broadly, something given or obtained gratuitously or by way of good measure. Every business can provide that something extra. It could be free shipping or a free sample of a new product. Service businesses could offer a free check-up, a training class, or a courtesy discount. A guest at Nashville's Opryland Resort inquired as to where she could get the spa-sound clock in her room. She learned that the product was made exclusively for the hotel, so she assumed that was the end of it. However, at the end of the day when she returned to her room, she found a gift with a handwritten note from the staff. They had given her one of the clocks. She was thrilled, and I can imagine became a customer for life. Take a moment to consider the culture, process, and training required to make that simple clock appear in that guest's room:

- Management had to recruit employees who work well with the public and provide them with consistent training.
- Management had to make customer "listening and responding" a part of the hotel's DNA.
- Employees had to have the authority to provide the item, the funding to pay for it, and the time to do something special for a customer.
- Employees had to know how to best present the clock.

I could probably make this list a bit longer, but the point is that your customers will not experience these kinds of memorable events by accident. The only things that happen by accident are, well, accidents.

- **Two Simple Words.** Your business shouldn't be transaction focused. It needs to be customer focused. That shift in attitude makes a significant difference because your interaction with the customer doesn't end when the purchase is completed. Saying thank you is so simple yet underused. When I asked my Facebook followers to share with me wonderful customer experiences, I got many answers I expected. But a new one jumped to the forefront: Chewy.com. When you register online with the pet-supply website, you get a handwritten thank you note via snail mail. Yes, you read this correctly: handwritten. You're also entered into a lottery to win an oil-painted portrait of your pet. As of this writing, approximately 15 percent of Chewy's employees are customer service representatives. They keep customer profiles and take copious notes so they get to know their customers and their pets. According to a December 2016 *Bloomberg Businessweek* article, the five-year-old company was on track to earn $880 million in revenue—definitely taking a bite out of its competitors and creating the One-Percent Edge.

Little things matter a lot when it comes to your customers and clients. Make sure you're focused on being better than good. Excel at providing that extra special touch so your business can soar to success.

Make It Easy to Do Business with You

Here are a few alarming statistics that you need to pay close attention to:

- Ninety-five percent of customers use three or more channels and devices to resolve a single customer service issue.
- One in five consumers who ended a business relationship because of poor customer service did so after waiting too long to talk to someone on the phone.
- Eighty-six percent of consumers describe a great customer service experience as one of the following: The company anticipates their needs, the self-service is optimal, or they're able to contact the company any way they want.
- Thirty-five percent of millennials report that optimal self-service is what they look for in a great customer service experience.

Recently, I listened to a small business owner talk about her start-up. She told a story about a Sunday evening when she was at home on her laptop, answering customer service questions. One of the customers told her how startled she was to get a response on a Sunday night.

This small business owner understands how important it is to get virtually immediate responses to customer service inquiries because that is the level of service she has come to expect. She said she is a member of the "Now Now Club." I think many of us have joined that club; we want our questions answered now and our problems solved now. Many Internet-based companies are doing such an incredible job at responding immediately and taking care of their customers that membership in the Now Now Club has become the norm.

You need to understand that this sword cuts two ways. First, if you please the Now Now Club, you can hold on to your customers for the long term. Providing incredible customer service along with a wonderful customer experience may be the two biggest weapons in your marketing campaign. They engender loyalty. People will pay a premium for them. You can be the high-price leader if you significantly outshine your competitors with your customer service.

About ten years ago, I created an online account using an email address I had at the time. A couple of years ago, when I tried to update the content in that account, I couldn't access anything. It said my username and password didn't match. So what do you do in those cases? You click on "I forgot my password." Of course, it then asked for the email address registered with the account. Big problem. I had no way of getting those emails, so I began trying to get help. I hunted through the "Help" area on the site. Nothing. I emailed via "Contact us." Nothing. Finally, I desperately searched for a phone number to talk to a real person. Nothing. I had no choice but to give up and start a new account.

Imagine if your customers have that kind of experience with your business. They want access to the help they need when they need it. Do you have the appropriate, varied, and flexible systems in place to handle customer questions, concerns, and complaints?

Gone are the days when you can define one entry point to your customer service system and plot a linear journey up the chain of command that your customer must travel to resolve issues. You see, the idea of business moving along a linear path is off point today. This especially applies to how your customers interact with your business. Picture your customers who have questions they need answered or problems that must be solved. They do not want to move through a linear help system; they want to pivot to the place where they can get their answers. They want to be able to turn immediately and find the resource that will solve their problem.

Here's what a [24]7 customer engagement survey found: Nearly two-thirds (64 percent) of all customer service inquiries start at a website. The first thing most people do is find a self-service system through which they can resolve their issues. If that doesn't deliver the desired results, they want to pivot immediately to a higher-level system that is convenient, such as an online chat system. Consumers don't want to plod along a trail that might eventually lead them to the answer they need; they want customer service system number two to be instantly available, at their fingertips.

"Companies need to provide robust self-service in the first channel and make it easy to get assistance and task completion in a second channel," the [24]7 survey concluded. "For companies this means that escalation from self-service channels (website or mobile app) to assisted-service channel (chat or phone), requires new capabilities in a world of effortless customer engagement. Chat and voice agents must be equipped with knowledge and context to understand what the customer did in prior channels."[9]

These "new capabilities" include artificial-intelligence-powered chatbots. Facebook is making a major play in this area with chatbot functionality in the Facebook Messenger app. This is an example of how artificial-intelligence technology is becoming increasingly accessible even to smaller businesses. Online chat has been a handy customer service tool for some years, but when it requires a warm body on the company side, we often get the "Chat Unavailable" message. Chatbots make this feature available 24/7.

Whatever mix of self-service, artificial intelligence, and human interaction you use, don't make your customers retell their tales of woe at every stop along their customer service journey.

The Personal Touch

I had a call from an American Airlines representative who was "checking in" to see how the airline was performing. First, I was surprised someone reached out to me unexpectedly. Second, I had a recent nightmare travel day that I was able to share with the rep. She apologized and agreed to add 10,000 frequent flier miles to my account and send a $100 travel voucher to me for my inconvenience. Wow.

Businesses collect a lot of customer satisfaction data from surveys, but if you truly want to know how you're doing, talk to your customers. If you have a product or service that involves many transactions being done online or with recurring charges, then, as the old AT&T commercial said, you need to reach out and touch someone.

A personal call from the owner or top-level manager can be far more beneficial in terms of getting the real story, especially when you've lost a customer or client. Make it clear that this is not a sales call intended to get the former subscriber to reup. Let the person know that you're just looking for ways to improve your product or service. In fact, you might offer a small gift card if the person will spend a few minutes on the phone with you. GoDaddy periodically calls account holders to measure their satisfaction with its performance.

Success today is closely tied to data collection and analysis, and that data needs to be lassoed so you can use it for improving customer service, products, and whatever is the focus of your business. However, the personal touch can go a long way in transforming one-time buyers into customers for life.

The VIP Customer

In Chapter 7, on creating the One-Percent Edge in your processes and systems, I note that while technology enhances every aspect of our business operations, customers long for high touch. We live in a world where it's difficult to connect to a human being, particularly in larger organizations.

Every customer and client wants to feel special. It's your job to make sure they get the VIP treatment. I go to certain restaurants because they know my name, remember my favorite dishes, and make me feel as though I'm their most important customer. Now, I know that isn't the case, but in a field as competitive as the restaurant business it is a critical edge.

At one of my favorites, Duffy's Sports Bar and Grille in Jupiter, Florida, I'm a "Hall of Famer" in their loyalty program. That means I get all sorts of special perks. So of course, like many of its customers, I go back time and time again.

Give exclusive deals and information to your VIP customers. One of the reasons I fly American Airlines consistently is because I'm a Platinum member for life. That means I don't get charged for checking a bag, I get priority boarding, I get to select the premium seating in coach for no charge, and I'm frequently upgraded to first class. That extra value is important to me as a business traveler.

The VIP treatment not only keeps customers loyal; it often results in strong word-of-mouth marketing. Word of mouth has always been one of the best ways to get new business, but it's even more important today with the advent of social media and review sites. Customers who are blown away by your business are likely to share it via their online communities. The magnitude of that reach is exponential.

Successful loyalty programs can increase revenue. For example, the Starbucks loyalty program originally gave customers a star for each transaction. Customers quickly figured out a way to rack up stars more quickly by asking baristas to ring up items individually. So executives changed the program to one that awards stars based on dollars spent, something customers had been requesting. Starbucks executives believe that the move will results in customers spending more, and Matthew Ryan, chief strategy officer at Starbucks, told the *Wall Street Journal* that most customers should also earn rewards more quickly.[10] A win-win situation.

CHAPTER 4

The Product Edge

"The man who comes up with a means of doing or producing almost anything better, faster or more economically has his future and his fortune at his fingertips."

—J. PAUL GETTY

A s you examine your product/service offerings with a critical eye, you must consider if there is dead weight among the mix that needs to be cut. As I noted when I explained how the One-Percent Edge process works, there can't be any sacred cows. It's a mistake to get married to a particular product or service.

- What is the pain in the market?
- Are our products/services still relevant to the market?
- Are there lucrative niches for our product?
- Can an online business offer features local businesses can't?
- Is our product at risk of becoming obsolete because of technology disruptions?
- What new competitive threats could affect our business?
- Are there collaborative opportunities with synergistic businesses?
- Are there new ways to market the business without jeopardizing profit and cash flow?
- Are there ways to improve our existing product or service?
- Have we become complacent? Are we married to our product/service offering?
- How can we meet the immediate gratification desires of today's customers?
- Are there new markets for our product?
- Are we hanging on to unprofitable products?
- Should we acquire another company or merge with one to gain market share and reach?

Cut the Dead Weight

When I graduated from college, IBM had the most-coveted jobs. It was clearly the market leader, and its office equipment and computers were second to none. However, as the world of personal computers evolved, Big Blue lost its footing. Competitors swamped the market with less-expensive options, and IBM was too big to respond quickly. In 1993, it posted the then-biggest loss in the history of corporate America: $8 billion.

With its back against the wall, IBM found itself in the unenviable position of having to innovate or die. The company's leadership made a tough call: It decided to abandon its long-time core business of hardware and instead focus on providing IT expertise and computing services to businesses. It also invested heavily in its server business, becoming the number one seller of enterprise server solutions in the world by 2013. The new IBM is also focused on data and analytic services as well as cloud platform solutions.

CEO Ginni Rometty writes in her 2015 report to investors that IBM "is the only company in our industry that has reinvented itself through multiple technology eras and economic cycles." The company has done that, she explains, to differentiate itself. The IT industry is transforming at record pace, and due to these changes, Rometty said, IBM is transforming into "a cognitive solutions and cloud platform company."[1]

Whether the century-old company will be able to sustain itself and its relevance remains to be seen. Letting go of the product side of its business in light of market changes had to have been a difficult decision. It's now the computer giant without the products it pioneered. Yet the market is moving in a different direction—it is changing—and IBM is doing its best to turn the ship in a new direction.

Despite the enormousness of this shift in its business model, it's important to realize that there is also an underlying consistency to what IBM is doing:

- It was a technology company yesterday.
- It is a service-technology company today.

To take that a little further, I also want to point out that IBM has always been in the business of selling "computing solutions" to customer problems. Yesterday, those solutions required hardware. Today, the hardware is almost irrelevant; handling big data is the computing problem that needs a solution.

Frankly, the customers to whom IBM markets its services today probably look about the same as the customers it sold high-powered computers to yesterday. This can be a critical element when a business decides it has to pivot to survive. We look more closely at what is required for a successful pivot or start-up at the end of this chapter and give you ideas and a framework to make those calls yourself.

A company with the One-Percent Edge must be willing to take a cold, hard look at its products and cut the dead weight before it's too late. Are you ready to reinvent your business?

Staying Relevant: Expand Your Customer Base

When you think of a typical Tesla Motors customer, you probably think of a somewhat geeked-out male. You would be right. According to *Businessweek*, when the company rolled out its Model S in 2012, only 13 percent of its customers were women. In an effort to meet aggressive sales goals, Tesla needs to attract more women drivers. Although women buy only 40 percent of all cars on the road in the United States, they make up 53 percent of the small SUV market, according to an analysis by J.D. Power and Associates. Prior to finalizing a design, the company conducted a focus group with women who drive SUVs and minivans to learn what they liked and didn't like about their current vehicles. Based on that feedback, in February 2012, the company unveiled the Model X. "With the S, we might be something like two-thirds male," Tesla founder Elon Musk said in an interview with Bloomberg. "With the X, I think we probably will be slightly majority female."[2]

Many of the examples I've shared so far throughout the book have talked about big brands; however, small businesses can succumb to irrelevancy too, and when that happens, the consequences often are much more severe. A small business that ignores the changing nature of the market and clings to its current business operations may be too far gone by the time the problem is identified. With little or no cash reserves and limited personnel, a small business may simply fade into the sunset. Think about your neighborhood video store. Most merely stood by as the video rental industry tanked. Consequently, their doors closed for good. Unfortunately, I had a good friend who purchased a video rental store at its peak but eventually went bankrupt because the market changed. That's why it is imperative for smaller firms to apply the One-Percent Edge process.

The increased use of voice recognition software and electronic medical records caused Denver-based Ben Walker's medical transcription business to begin struggling. "I recognized it, but I kind of refused to fully recognize it," he said. However, as more clients in the medical field began to drop off, rather than sit on his hands and watch his business dwindle, Walker created a new company, Transcription Outsourcing, and expanded his target market. In the past, he had received queries from law enforcement agencies, lawyers and courthouses, universities, and researchers. So he spent time researching these markets, learning about their needs, and how they do business. Soon he was responding to RFPs—requests for proposals—and began to add clients in these new markets.

Big Data Helps Take the Guesswork
Out of Decision Making

In determining your product strategy, the data you collect can help take the guesswork out of your decisions. However, you must look at data with an open mind and be agile enough to adjust your strategy accordingly.

In four decades, fashion brand Zara has grown from a single store in La Coruna, Spain, into the biggest fashion retailer on earth. Interestingly, there is no bureaucratic hierarchy at this shop. The company's 350 or so designers, guided by daily data feeds showing what's selling and what's stalling, each has a say in the final designs. They monitor sales figures and thousands of comments from customers, store managers, and country directors. Armed with that information, the company's teams go to work to develop products for the coming weeks.

Zara's parent company, Iditex, is enjoying significant success while other retailers are struggling. "There is no magic formula," said Pablo Isla, Inditex's chairman and chief executive officer. "There are no stars. We are able to react to data during the season, but in the end, what we offer our customers is fashion, and there's a human element to that."[3] Another element of Zara's success is its ability to generate ideas from customers in real time. This is completely contrary to the model of most fashion houses, which design fashions at least two seasons ahead and then push the collections on consumers.

Today's business world operates in real time, and big data is the answer to helping business leaders stay in sync with markets. Big data helps brands individualize the customer experience by tracking information that affects the customer experience. Data mining also gives your business the opportunity to determine what the customer wants to improve interactions.

Listen to the Patient

> "Businesses come up with a specific format, or a specific product or process. They fall so in love with themselves that they don't listen to what the consumer wants, and they become obsolete. . . . They don't anticipate tomorrow."
>
> **—MARCUS LEMONIS of CNBC Prime's *The Profit***

When business leaders examine numbers, they can serve as a mechanism to rationalize a conclusion. So as a cautionary note, using big data is a good way to measure market trends and customer behavior, but it doesn't eliminate the need to put your ear to the ground and listen. My doctor believes in looking at test results, but he recognizes the importance of also listening to the patient. The same is true when you're building your business strategy.

Does Your Product Have Just a Noticeable Difference?

> "A lot of times, people don't know what they want until you show it to them."
>
> **—STEVE JOBS**

Back in 1978, a couple of guys who had been friends since junior high school were floundering around trying to get their careers off the ground. They were hitting a lot of dead ends. Because this was the 1970s, I suppose we would say that they were trying to "find themselves." With no luck getting started on a traditional career path, they decided to create their own jobs and went into business for themselves. Of course, neither one knew anything about starting a business, but that didn't deter them. Nor were they discouraged by the fact they had no idea what type of business to start. After some discussion, they chose the food business because they both liked to eat—and more specifically, the ice cream business, because they loved ice cream.

The two then invested in a $5 correspondence course from Penn State University that taught them how to make ice cream. Next they combined their life savings and acquired a bank loan totaling $12,000. On May 5, 1978, they opened their ice cream shop in an abandoned gas station in Burlington, Vermont.

By now, I know you've figured out I'm talking about Ben Cohen and Jerry Greenfield of Ben & Jerry's fame. But Ben and Jerry's story could have wound up like most business owners and we wouldn't be here talking about them today. They could have served up some pretty awesome scoops of vanilla, strawberry, chocolate, and maybe a little butter pecan to spice it up. Perhaps they would have made a fairly decent living for themselves and their families. Who knows, they might have opened up a few more locations. All in all, however, it would have been a rather unexceptional story.

That's what most of us in business do: We follow the same path and produce pretty much the same product or service as everyone else, and our business becomes a commodity. Plus, we get caught up in the day-to-day management, often becoming so consumed by it that we ignore opportunities to innovate. Instead of following the tried-and-true path, Ben and Jerry decided to shake things up.

You see, Ben Cohen had a condition called anosmia, the inability to perceive odor. He relied on what's known as mouth feel when he ate. So the new entrepreneurs threw in all sorts of funky ingredients in big chunks to create what I like to call a "just noticeable difference." That noticeable difference paid off. Soon there was a line of customers waiting to get into that little ice cream store in Burlington, Vermont. Why? Because Ben and Jerry offered something consumers couldn't get anywhere else. They gave people a reason to change their buying habits. They filled a void in the market by offering something new.

Clearly, Ben and Jerry didn't invent ice cream. Ice cream had been around since colonial days. George Washington, Ben Franklin, and Thomas Jefferson were fans. Dolley Madison insisted it be served at the inaugural ball of her husband, James. Ben and Jerry's recipes are basically the same ingredients that have been used for centuries: milk or cream, some flavoring, and of course, sugar. But they discovered their "secret sauce" for that "just noticeable difference." Plus, they insisted their products be all natural and friendly to the earth and environment, which is another noticeable difference. (See more on the importance of purpose in Chapter 5, "The People Edge.")

Ironically, my favorite flavor of Ben & Jerry's ice cream is Cherry Garcia, which was named after the Grateful Dead's Jerry Garcia, who once said, "It's not enough to be the best at what you do; you must be perceived to be the only one who does what you do."

Similarly, the success of Apple was the result of creating a noticeable difference as opposed to "inventing" technology. Apple didn't invent personal computers, but it enhanced them by creating an intuitive, icon-based interface and offering products in sleeker designs. The same is true with MP-3 players. There were other products on the market when Apple introduced its iPod. Sales soared because of the unique design; and instead of black earplugs, the iPod had white ones, which became a kind of social-style statement.

Can you truly say there is a difference between your product and your competitor's? Don't believe your own company's marketing spin. Drill down. Do an objective analysis. Can your customers get basically what you offer from your competitor? Why would they choose you over another business? Answering these questions with confidence is the One-Percent Edge.

Distribution, New Markets

Distribution channels are changing. It's much easier to interface directly with a customer. Historically, a new product such as a salad dressing would have to compete aggressively for shelf space against established brands. Not only was it difficult to get the distribution, but it was expensive. Today, all types of brands can connect directly with their customers via the Internet.

P&G has always relied on retailers to sell its products. Enter Dollar Shave Club in 2012—no frills, great razors for a low subscription price, delivered right to your doorstep—and the brand powerhouse was caught by surprise. The start-up significantly changed the buying habits of the marketplace. According to a *Wall Street Journal* article, Gillette (owned by P&G) has lost U.S. market share for six straight years. Its share of the men's-razors business fell to 54 percent in 2016 from 59 percent in 2015.[4]

As a result, P&G began to focus on how consumers buy today, hoping to limit the impact of more-innovative start-ups that were trying to capture part of its market. The company launched the Gillette Shave Club to compete head-to-head with Dollar Shave. In Atlanta, P&G launched an online subscription service for its Tide Pods capsules, the highest priced laundry detergent among its product offerings. In Chicago, customers can use a smartphone app to order laundry pickup and delivery from cars branded with the Tide logo.

Although P&G management was probably aware of the upstart company, it wasn't asking the right questions. Its framework for analysis was lodged in dated business methods and models. The company is now hiring more workers with entrepreneurial backgrounds to help it address changing markets and competition.

Piggyback Opportunities

A friend of mine likes to watch the gold-mining shows on cable television. He recently noted that the miners are lucky to break even each year, but the guys who lease heavy equipment and sell replacement parts are making out like bandits.

That story is as old as the California Gold Rush, which played an important role in giving us brands like Levi Strauss, Armour meats, and Wells Fargo, and it continues to be played out today, even with some high-tech twists.

In a concept called piggybacking, the goal is to find a fast-growing start-up or a new sector and then to develop a service that makes it easier to use or more profitable.

From Mom to Millionaire

A piggyback idea sparked in the basement of a Colorado home turned a stay-at-home mom into a millionaire. Sheri Schmelzer started creating fun decorations for her children's Crocs, and soon other youngsters wanted them too. Originally the company, which she named Jibbitz, was launched as a website. Demand grew quickly. Within six months, Jibbitz grew from $200,000 to $2 million and caught the attention of the leadership at Crocs. The company acquired Jibbitz for $10 million, and today you'll find Crocs Jibbitz shoe charms and embellishments as part of the Crocs product offerings.

eBay Offshoots

Were you around when eBay launched? If so, you may have noticed that it didn't take long for a whole bevy of businesses to get started that made it easier to post or track your items. As eBay grew, so did the demand for these ancillary businesses.

This phenomenon will continue. If you are looking for a business idea, keep tabs on where the venture capital is going and watch the business pages for stories about start-up trends. If you've been following the trends, you will know that peer-to-peer enterprises are hot today. Consequently, this area is experiencing a lot of piggybacking.

Services to manage your Airbnb listings are being established, for example. How many homeowners really know what their room should rent for or want to deal with booking and cleaning the rentals? This could give local house cleaning companies an area into which they can expand.

Breeze started out leasing cars to Uber and Lyft wannabe drivers who lacked wheels. But then Lyft and Uber established partnerships that allowed them to lease vehicles themselves. This points out one of the dangers of going all in on a piggybacking venture: Eventually the big player in the game, if there is one, may decide to provide the service itself. Plus, there's always the possibility that the company or industry on which you are piggybacking might fall out of favor, making your idea a very risky venture.

New Laws Make New Businesses

Just as the creation of a new business model can create piggybacking opportunities in the private sector, new laws can create new business opportunities in the public sector. The upheaval in healthcare caused by the Affordable Care Act created demand for a wide range of new services, such as converting records to a digital format and payments processing.

However, even beyond that, all the newly insured patients flocking to hospitals and clinics are causing significant business growth in many parts of our country. Traditional services, even basic needs such as janitorial, can piggyback on the growth resulting from the law.

At the end of each year, you may have noticed that local media start publishing articles on all the new laws that will take effect in the coming year. Make it your pre-New Year's resolution to seek these out and see if the new laws will create demand for a new product or service and then explore ways to be the best provider of those.

With all of this in mind, be alert to the changes happening around you, whether they are new businesses, new social phenomena, or new laws. With each of these, demand is being created for new products and services that are complementary.

Everything Old Can Be New Again

I believe that politics is the only profession that gets less respect than used car sales. Taking a fresh look at the used car industry, New York-based Vroom is working to rid it of its traditional hassles and haggling, and bring the commerce online. Unlike some of its competitors that match buyers with sellers, Vroom actually purchases its cars, refurbishes them, and guarantees them, minimizing the risk of making such a large purchase via the Internet. According to a *Bloomberg Businessweek* article, the company sold tens of thousands of cars last year, generating about $900 million in revenue. Operations are powered by proprietary technology programs, which give the company the ability to move inventory quickly.

Another age-old business is teaching piano lessons. I did it to earn money when I was in high school. I don't want to give private piano lessons a bad rap here. However, I know that many youngsters find piano lessons a dull chore, and I also know that later in life, many adults wish they had studied piano, or tried harder when they had lessons in their youth. (A market void?)

One of the best things about technology today is that it can help us learn things we missed earlier in life. Technology does this by making learning more convenient and less expensive. Sometimes it can also customize content delivery in ways that better suit our individual learning styles. In fact, I think one of the most exciting areas today is in learning technology, or e-learning. You can't watch television without seeing a commercial for an online university, for example.

One of the newest and best examples in this area is Skoove, an online and very tech-savvy piano teaching system. I think it can get more kids playing piano and also fulfill the dreams of many adults by providing them with a convenient way to learn fundamental piano skills.

For the kids, working with a computer and Internet connection is probably more in line with how they prefer to spend their time. For adults, being able to learn piano in the privacy of their homes and whenever they have the time are major selling points.

"[Sixty-one] percent of the people in the US, UK, Australia, and Germany would like to learn a musical instrument, but currently only a fraction actually do. With Skoove, we hope to make that dream a reality for anyone with access to a computer and a desire to learn," said Florian Plenge, Skoove cofounder and CEO.[5]

Riches in the Niches

The answer to staying relevant could be narrowing your focus. That may sound counterintuitive, but the research shows that when you identify and attract a particular niche, you'll enjoy greater customer loyalty. Think of it as creating a captive community where your business is the go-to provider.

There are many online resources for sending flowers to that special person. Probably the best known is 1-800-Flowers. So instead of being a sheep and following the flock, Dirty Rotten Flowers took an opposite approach: As its name implies, you can send a wilted bouquet to someone that says, "Thanks for nothing." One bouquet is called "I love you, not."

Here are a few satisfied customer testimonials from its website:

"When my future daughter-in-law conveniently uninvited me to my son's birthday event, I sent her Dirty Rotten Flowers. She's not speaking to me . . . exactly what I hoped for. . . . Thank you DRF."

—Catherine, 65, wife and mother

"My girlfriend literally left me a 'dear John' note after I left for the office. She's now shacked up with her trainer. I sent her the Morticia bouquet . . . and got the last word."

—Jonathan, 32, computer programmer

"I sent Dirty Rotten Flowers anonymously to a casting agent after I didn't get a callback and it felt awesome!"

—Jasmine (not my real name), 23, actress

It's amazing what business opportunities you can uncover when you have an open mind and strive to take an innovative approach. And by the way, these nonblossoms aren't cheap. The Dirty Rotten bouquet runs $33 for what is literally a vase of dead flowers.

Finding a niche limits your pool of competitors. However, you must do the necessary research to ensure that your niche is large enough to sustain your business. The risk is going too narrow with a niche or too broad. So using the One-Percent Edge process of analyzing your opportunities, prioritize those that are the most likely candidates and then continue to review, measure, and adjust.

When Steve Jobs said that people don't know what they want until you show it to them, I considered the idea brilliant. But because it came from Jobs, I framed it in terms of the big, mass-market product categories where he was such a driving force. After I began to explore the nature of niche markets, I saw that the idea he was expressing relates directly to creating these powerful and lucrative slices of the commercial pie. One of the most important attributes of a niche market is that it doesn't preexist; it needs to be created.

You can identify a niche market for yourself with consumers or in a B2B sector. For success, one of the most important requirements is that your product or service is unique, so that people must go to you to get it.

Further, you need to be able to clearly define who your customers are. If you can't do this, you can't reach them. While this is important in any market, it's even more so in a niche market. When your product or service appeals to a broad market segment, you can be less precise in your marketing and advertising campaigns and still achieve some degree of success. But when you know that your market is small to begin with, any misfires in your marketing and advertising will deliver two bad results:

- You'll spend a lot of money.
- You won't make any sales.

We want win-wins, not double whammies. If you don't know who your customers are, don't go any further with your business idea.

And that brings us to the question of how to come up with solid niche market ideas. Let's touch base with the two concepts we've already discussed:

- The niche market definition makes it clear that these markets are created.
- You must be able to identify your customers.

If you want to build a business, product, or service around a niche market, it's good to start with what you already know. Consider your company's expertise and core competencies, and then approach the question from two sides, the product or service and the market:

- Can you make changes to your product or service that would create new opportunities?
- Can your product or service be used in ways that differ from what you now consider its main function?
- Is there an unserved market? If so, where? Here? Abroad?
- Are there inconveniences for a specific market segment that you could address?

If you can develop a unique product or service in an area that's close to you, you have a good chance to succeed. You will be in a position to judge the value of your creation—its marketability—and you'll also know who your market is. That's a winning combination.

Let me add one final bonus of setting your sights on developing a niche market: Because you know who you need to sell to, you can conduct smaller, inexpensive tests to gauge your probability of success. And if you succeed, you'll be in a position to write the next successful chapter of your business!

A Niche Market Warning

You may remember my comments in the chapter on the Customer Edge about Fox founding two Spanish-language cable channels. One was a news channel that folded, and the other was a sports channel. It's interesting to note how Fox changed the name (brand) of its sports channel. It started out as Fox Sports en Español (Fox Sports in Spanish) and was changed to Fox Deportes (Fox Sports).

There is an important lesson here: When you create a product or service for a niche market, it shouldn't seem to the consumer like a second-hand version of some other product or service you market to another (and probably more important) group of buyers. That shows disrespect for the niche group, and it ignores a marketing fact of life today: People are looking for authenticity.

If you or your company comes off as phony, shallow, or opportunistic, you won't be able to build the kind of relationship you need to sustain your business in the desired niche. The original name, Fox Sports en Español, sent the message that the channel was something of an afterthought, like English subtitles on a French film; it wasn't an authentic Spanish-language endeavor from the company. I'm sure that Fox had every intention to do a great job programming sports that would appeal to this audience, but its original branding didn't exactly convey that message.

Go in a Different Direction

> "If everybody is doing it one way, there's a good chance you
> can find your niche by going exactly in the opposite
> direction."
>
> —SAM WALTON

Why go after the same customers as your competition? What audience are they missing? No business is going to appeal to everyone. How are you going to capture those customers who have little or no interest in your competitor's offerings? This could be a complete shift in your operations or a new vertical.

Furniture can be an expensive purchase, particularly for young people just starting out. Many, including myself, accepted hand-me-downs or shopped for deals at consignment stores. If you were lucky enough to hit a big sale at one of the established retail venues, you'd have to wait for the product to be delivered and most likely pay extra for that service, unless you had someone with a truck to help.

The founder of Ikea, Ingvar Kamprad, identified this market problem and decided to make it his mission to offer a wide range of well-designed, functional, affordable home furnishing products. And so you didn't have to wait for the dealer to schedule your delivery, he developed the flat-packing system so customers could take home and assemble the furniture the same day they purchased it.

The concept was a big hit, and the company grew quickly. Kamprad identified a market void and went in the opposite direction of the entire furniture industry. As a result, Ikea grew to be the behemoth we know today. According to its website, as of June 2017 there are more than 390 IKEA stores in 48 countries.

The company continues to keep that entrepreneurial, innovative spirit. One of its listed values is "Daring to be different." It accomplishes this by questioning old solutions, identifying better ideas, and being willing to change. Ikea also promotes the need to review what was done today and consider how it could be done better tomorrow.

March to Your Own Drummer

Every season the fashion industry unveils new trends and styles. You may love shoulder pads, but if you wear them today you'll probably get a few puzzled glances. The industry icons want to dictate to you what to wear and how to wear it.

Bucking that trend, the founders of Lunch at the Ritz earrings, Esme Hecht and Zander Elliott, say they founded the jewelry company for women who could care less about what the fashion magazines say and more about their own independent style. Three-plus decades later, the company is still going strong. Each piece of jewelry has a theme; each is a limited edition work of art. For example, I own a pair of New Year's Eve earrings, which of course are part of my festive attire. You can find almost anything you're interested in—wine, shopping, law, theater, holidays—you name it. And even though Lunch at the Ritz is costume jewelry, it's not inexpensive. Prices start around $100. I have quite a few pieces. You have to be confident about your personal style to wear them. Not everyone will understand your choice.

The brand's popularity created collectors who clamor for discontinued pieces. Just take a quick look on eBay and you'll see the demand for discontinued Lunch at the Ritz items. Prices range from fifty to several hundred dollars

According to the company's website, its secret to remaining relevant in a highly competitive and ever-changing market is never to look at what someone else is doing, break all the rules, and be true to yourself. I've said many times that if you're jumping on the bandwagon today you're too late. Establishing a unique niche and understanding your customer are critical elements of the One-Percent Edge.

Changing Old Habits

Earlier I noted that change for change's sake is never the answer. An organization that thinks making sweeping changes will deter its demise is simply desperate. Remember the case study with RadioShack, a company that changed nearly every time the wind changed, resulting in market confusion and a complete loss of its core customers.

However, sometimes change is inevitable. For example, Netflix recognized that the mail-order DVD business was dying. So it transitioned its business into a video streaming service. In making such a major change in its business platform, however, it helped to educate its customers along the way so they would feel comfortable with the new product offering. I think for most of us it's always easier to adjust to incremental enhancements than to an abrupt departure. Video streaming was foreign to many of the company's customers, yet by helping those customers transition, the company maintained its relevancy and continues to be a successful business today.

Adapting to Technology Disruption

Change in response to new technology happens frequently and quickly. We've all seen it. Soon after technologies appear on the scene, some companies disappear because they lacked the ability to adapt accordingly. Others find ways to adjust and remain relevant in the face of changing realities.

There is probably no better example of technology making a company's foundational core competency obsolete than Western Union. In its heyday, Western Union reportedly sent out more than 200 million telegrams a year. When long-distance phone service became affordable, the business declined, and the Internet pounded the last nail into the telegram's coffin. However, the company remains relevant today. It is the world's largest money transfer service, with more than 515,000 agent locations in 200 countries.

Digitron Electronics, based in Montebello, California, is in the audiovisual repair business. Recognizing the demise of the small repair shops, its leaders looked for ways to remain relevant. The company began to create alliances with major manufacturers that were downsizing their own technical staffs. Then it developed a team that specialized in the repair and maintenance of broadcast video cameras, decks, and monitors. It meant the company had to cut dead weight and quit servicing some brands that didn't pay enough for services to make it a profitable business. The change in direction resulted in attracting clients such as Walt Disney Studios, Cirque Du Soleil, Panasonic, and the U.S. military.

Another industry that has been significantly impacted by disruptive technology is the newspaper business. Many of the names we once knew have disappeared. In my hometown of St. Louis, *The Globe Democrat* is gone and the St. Louis *Post Dispatch* that once published twice a day is down to a morning paper only. Personally, I read the news on my iPad. It beats getting black ink on my hands and wrestling with the folds. The news outlets that are doing better than their competitors are the ones that have embraced the new technology. For example, the *Wall Street Journal* has a robust online publication that is updated regularly throughout the day. Readers have a choice of subscribing to either the print or online publications, or both.

The bottom line when it comes to technology disruption is that it isn't going away. Business leaders need to continually evaluate the risks and stay poised to pivot. As they say, if you can't beat them, join them.

Go Wider: Mass Customization

This may sound counterintuitive to many of you after my previous discussion about niche markets: While we know that "one size fits all" is seldom, if ever, true, we know that in sales, the more people who are good fits for our products and services, the more profitable we'll be.

This fundamental truth has created what we call mass customization, a strategy that everyone from retailers on Etsy to huge B2B manufacturers are doing. The term is something of an oxymoron, but if you can wrap your brain around the concept, you can put your business on the path to better sales.

While there are four different approaches to mass customization, let me start with a simple illustration. Imagine an e-commerce site that designs and sells music education materials, such as learning how to play the blues. A guitar player may have written the original course with other guitar players in mind.

Since the heart of the teaching materials applies to a wide variety of instruments, the business owner decides to pursue other market segments, such as piano players. But he soon discovers that his guitar-blazoned teaching materials and all the guitar talk on the website are turnoffs to piano players.

Changing the Look

While the core information doesn't change, the business owner produces a version of his course that includes keyboard graphics. He even creates a microsite that is designed totally around pianos and keyboards. He tweaks the email marketing materials so they are customized for guitar players, keyboard players, and eventually even saxophone players and others.

Of the four approaches to mass customization, this one would fall into the cosmetic category: The core product remains the same, but its appearance is changed to appeal to different market segments. To pull off this kind of customization successfully, you need to segment your prospects precisely so they get into the right sales funnel; and then be sure they receive the right follow-on offers after they become customers.

A good cloud-based, small business, customer-relationship-management system will handle this. The challenge will be for advertising and marketing to find the right prospects. In my music-teaching example, advertising channels such as AdWords or, perhaps even better, Facebook ads, would help the business owner target people who play the right instruments and are open to learning.

As I explained, my example is basically cosmetic. However, there are others that are more substantial. A friend of mine bought an inflatable kayak he uses for fishing. The kayak itself comes in a basic package, however it's available in a variety of configurations depending on whether you want to use it for fishing or navigating whitewater.

Adapting for Special Uses

This is adaptive mass customization. Your business starts with a basic product, and the customers get add-ons to make it suit their specific uses. In the software world, we see programs with functions that can be customized by adding various plug-ins.

With this approach, not only do you need to deal with prospect and customer segmentation as discussed above, but you also have significant supply-chain challenges. With my kayak example, you need to order the specially adapted angler seat in the right numbers and at the right time; increased production for the holiday season is probably required.

When significant investments are required for manufacturing and inventorying products, understanding the customer and product life cycles is critical. Being able to mine historic industry data and make good predictions can be the difference between posting a profit or a loss.

Sticking to Core Competencies with a New Direction

I've told you about a start-up that piggybacked on the initial success of Crocs, but what about the company itself? It went through a time when its prospects looked rather bleak.

This clunky (and in my opinion ugly) functional, affordable, comfortable footwear made from a type of molded plastic took the market by storm. Sales soared quickly, and in just over two years, the company went public. But as is true for many shooting stars, it fizzled out quickly, and its stock price tanked. Originally, Crocs were sold only in boutique stores or shopping mall kiosks, but eventually you could stop at your local 7-11 and pick up a pair along with your Big Gulp. The once popular shoes lost their "cool" factor. In fact, if you Google "hate crocs," you'll discover post after post trashing the brand.

How would you revive such a brand? I certainly wasn't in the boardroom when the Crocs leadership began to ponder this question, but I can confidently speculate about what was considered. One option might be to hire celebrities to sport the shoes in advertisements and public appearances. It could help in regaining the favor of their lost customers. However, such a tactic isn't guaranteed and would be extremely expensive.

Alternatively, the company could have chosen to pour a significant amount of money into R&D in order to develop another groundbreaking product. Of course, that takes time and money.

The company needed to stick to what it did well: manufacturing functional, affordable, and comfortable footwear, but with a new twist. So it launched new lifestyle shoes that range from sneakers and golf shoes to leopard-print ballet flats. In fact, I have a pair of those and I love them, whereas I wouldn't have been caught dead in the original Crocs.

Recognizing your core competency and adapting it to market trends is a smart business strategy and can help you maintain your relevancy.

Peanut Butter and Jelly

Who would have ever thought about putting those two products together? One sticks to the roof of your mouth, while the other is sweet and squishy. Yet, when combined with white bread, they become PB&J, and the result is explosive. A survey commissioned by jelly maker J.M. Smucker Company found that the average American eats more than 1,500 PB&J sandwiches before graduating from high school.

Think about the effect on each product's individual sales. Combining one with the other broadens the market exponentially. Further, PB&J unlocked opportunities for creative entrepreneurs with another simple tweak. In 1999, two independent inventors, Len Kretchman and David Geske, were granted a patent for a sealed crustless sandwich consisting of peanut butter and jelly with a long shelf life. Smucker bought the patent from the inventors and developed a commercial product, Uncrustables, based on it. Today, the company sells over $60 million of Uncrustables a year. A simple change created a new distribution channel. And the reinvention of the PB&J continues as gourmet restaurants introduce fancy versions on their menus. Street vendors deep-fry them. Pancake houses offer them up as waffles.

As you reflect on your business strategy, ask if there is a peanut butter for your jelly. Collaboration can produce new and broader market opportunities.

Working with the Customer

For many items, in both the consumer and B2B markets, companies use collaborative mass customization. In these situations, usually a salesperson helps the end buyer get the appropriate bells and whistles.

In an article for the *Harvard Business Review*, James H. Gilmore and B. Joseph Pine II point to Japanese eyewear retailer Paris Miki. The company has a computer-based system that allows customers to see how various frames would look on their faces, and it also discusses the requirements of the lenses they need. When the customer and vision professional hit the right look with the right lens, the system sends the information automatically to the lens grinder.[6]

Anticipating Requirements

The fourth type of mass customization—if I may be so bold—is when your supplier knows more about what you need than you do. Let's say a commercial soap manufacturer formulates the company's product to match varying degrees of water hardness around the nation. The end buyer might not even realize this, but when compared to a soap that wasn't custom formulated, the user notices the superiority.

In this scenario, you must have in place a solid system that regulates production and recognizes where product is being shipped. You can also employ surveys that ask about usage and special circumstances to make sure products are being shipped that best match the end use and location.

With all the data we have available today, there are many opportunities for customization—if we are wise enough to first mine that data, create the custom products and services, and then put the systems in place to be sure that we are maintaining tight operational controls.

Changing Demands

For nearly a decade, I worked in the financial services world in a division that specialized in a type of asset-based lending known as floor planning. You're probably familiar with this from the automobile industry, but we provided the same type of financing for dealers in myriad industries, from motorcycles and RVs to computers and office equipment. As long as a product from a manufacturer had a serial number, we could create finance programs for the dealer.

Periodically, floor checkers would visit the dealers' locations and take inventory to make sure the product we financed (which was our collateral) was still on the floor. For many years, this business was a cash cow, but slowly it began to lose its value. Why? The onset of just-in-time inventory. Dealers no longer needed to finance showroom and warehouse inventory.

Today, businesses and consumers are turning to fast-delivery options. With one click you can order food for delivery from your favorite restaurant, order an in-home yoga instructor, or even get your hair and makeup done at your office on demand before an evening out. Complete meal kits arrive at the doorsteps of busy professionals who want to eat healthier but hate to shop for ingredients.

While technology may open new ways to meet your customers' demands, it also poses challenges for business leaders. How do you maintain the connection to your market? Are there ways you can provide a tiered approach to your customer experience? The tension here is between the desire for a fast, real-time response (point and click) and a more detailed, involved, or upscale, direct interaction (sit down and talk about it). The One-Percent Edge positions you to analyze these nuances to adjust appropriately and still preserve your customer relationship.

Find the Niche, Tailor the Offering

There are two ways to begin your approach to identifying a niche market relationship: from the product side or from the market side. Most of our discussion so far has been from the side of product development, so now let's look at a strategy to identify the potential for niche market relationships from the market side.

I've tried to give you an appreciation for the diversity that exists in the market. Our demographics are sliced and diced more today than ever before. To take advantage of this, I suggest you create a spreadsheet with all the demographic segments of the U.S. market entered down the left-hand column. Each of these groups represents a potential niche market. Once you think you have all the groups identified, list all your products and services across the top of your spreadsheet.

Next, brainstorm how your product or service can be customized for every cell in the spreadsheet you have created. For example, if you sold house paints, there would be a cell in your spreadsheet for millennial immigrants from Latin America. You might do some research on the color preferences for this group of buyers and then pull together special color palettes to use in your marketing that targets this demographic.

There will be, of course, some cells where you're at a loss to identify anything you can do differently to make your product or service especially appealing to that niche market. Generation Z, for example, may be too young to be thinking about house paints.

This exercise shows how diversity on your team can greatly enhance your business's future growth. Don't brainstorm in isolation. Bring as many others on your team into the process as possible. When people with a wide range of backgrounds are trying to solve this puzzle, it's likely they will bring valuable insights into groups of which you have little knowledge or understanding.

Global Growth Can Build Sustainability

You can take this idea even further by adapting your products to global markets. Ninety-five percent of the world's purchasing power lies outside the U.S. borders. For those of you who are leaders in large organizations, you may already be tapping into international markets. But small and midsize businesses might not be taking advantage of this growth opportunity. According to the U.S. Small Business Administration, less than 1 percent of America's nearly 30 million small businesses are involved in exporting. And a study by the Institute for International Economics found that U.S. companies that export not only grow faster but also are nearly 8.5 percent less likely to go out of business than nonexporting companies.[7]

Global growth presents opportunities for established brands, growth organizations, and small businesses. Technology has really changed the game for small businesses that in the past lacked the resources or expertise to expand into global markets.

The founders of Dream Beard, Ryan and Brittany Lane, started their business, which provides products for men's facial hair, on Brittany's father's dining room table. The company was among the first of its kind, and it grew quickly. Four months after the Lanes started, they were selling products in over thirty-five countries. "If you are in ecommerce, I would ask 'Why not?' Why not cast your net into bigger waters?" said Ryan Lane.

Although we read about the daily give and take regarding international trade issues, such as major trade agreements between various groups of nations, the course of history is clear: Global trade will continue to increase.

Leaders implementing the One-Percent Edge process will find ways to benefit from global trade. Expanding beyond our borders not only opens new markets for you but can also help buffer market downturns. Sales may decrease in the United States but be hot in Asia or vice versa.

Fluctuations in the value of the major international currencies can also impact your business. We have seen some large corporations benefit and be harmed by changes in the value of the dollar relative to other currencies. If you buy supplies or materials that are imported, you can help protect yourself against a weak dollar by selling overseas.

To be in a position to take advantage of a weaker dollar, you must have a presence overseas. If you wait until the time looks "perfect," it will be too late. If you take the steps now to see how other economies are developing and how other cultures operate, you may find that your product or service is a good fit, or could be a good fit with some minor alterations.

Americans are in the enviable position of being the pop culture leaders of the world. While we might not export television sets any more, the world wants the clothes we wear, the music we listen to, and all kinds of consumer items. Go to the most distant village on earth and you'll find Coca-Cola for sale. I recently heard about a young woman who is buying overstock or discontinued women's clothing here, boxing it up, and shipping it to sales reps in the jungles of Bolivia. It's a small operation, but the concept could be applied in a larger setting.

Becoming a Self-Learner: The Art of the Pivot

In many ways, the Internet is the great equalizer. I've talked about how it enables smaller businesses to compete with much larger companies. It's also a great equalizer because it has lowered the barriers to entry for many businesses.

Couple this lower barrier to entry with the speed at which businesses evolve today and it creates an environment that accelerates the rate at which individuals are founding businesses and existing business owners are pivoting their business models.

On the popular reality-TV fashion-design show *Project Runway*, Heidi Klum opens each episode saying, "As you know in fashion, one day you're in. And the next day, you're out." It's the same for any business. In recent decades, the length of time a firm will spend on the Fortune 500 list has decreased dramatically.

The challenge when founding or pivoting a business is to make sure that the next day you aren't out.

Throughout this chapter, I've given you a lot of examples of successful business models as well as failures. Review them to understand the lessons they teach. They will increase your odds for success when you start a new business or need to change the course of your current one, in other words: pivot.

The question is, "Why do some business ideas have a good run and others fizzle?" While there is no simple answer (at least when you're trying to make predictions), you can improve your odds if you study past failures and successes and look for patterns or commonly shared attributes. In fact, I suggest you keep notes on failures and successes among pivots and start-ups. Make yourself assign a cause for the eventual outcome. Here are a few that I believe illustrate important points.

> *Banana Republic.* Does the name of this clothing store chain sound odd to you? If you knew its origins, it wouldn't. Originally, the company sold what was essentially safari or

safari-inspired clothing. Its big item was a photographer's vest that had about a dozen pockets to hold lenses.

I believe that the novelty of that retail model wore thin. Gap bought it out and rebranded it as an upscale clothing store that seems to be going fairly strong today.

What can we grab onto here to determine why the original idea ran out of steam but the pivot has proven staying power? The key is in the word *novelty*. A novelty idea can get off to an extremely fast start, but by definition, the sense of novelty erodes over time. However, there will always be demand for upscale clothes.

Webvan. This company is the poster child for the first wave of megadotcom failures during the historic bursting of the original dotcom bubble. The core idea was home grocery delivery. The idea sounded so good, but it crashed and burned in magnificent fashion.

What went wrong? I believe the basic reason behind its failure belongs in the "Before its time" column. However, the size of its failure can be explained by attempting to take an unproven idea too far too fast. In other words, smaller trials should have convinced company leaders and investors that their idea was ahead of its time.

PayPal. This ubiquitous Internet payment method started out hoping to sell a digital security system for personal digital assistants (PDAs) that would let users beam payments—think early version of Apple Pay, more or less. But the potential users weren't a big demographic, not to mention that this was back in the days when such a payment method would have required a ridiculously high level of trust.

The company pivoted to a more general, web-based payment system. This offered several advantages from a business launch point of view. First, it could ride the same wave that e-commerce in general was riding. Second, PayPal could develop a standardized system that would work on all browsers. With the earlier PDA concept, the company would have to deal with various brands of PDAs, as well as diverse and evolving operating systems.

Let me share one more pivot-in-progress that a friend told me about. A few companies have recently developed smartphone apps that serve a function similar to AAA's roadside assistance service. One of these companies started out by marketing to consumers, which seemed logical. After all, there are millions of drivers out there, and you would think that a lot of them would go for the idea.

However, concentrating on individual consumers means you have to make a lot of single sales. The company my friend told me about has pivoted and is now marketing its app/service to insurance companies. It has basically moved from being founded in B2C to concentrating on B2B. This makes defining its prospects much easier. Is it a major insurer? If yes, then let's put together a proposal. American drivers are a diverse population. Selling to those folks would be a real challenge; drivers in general are sort of the ultimate anti-niche market.

Recognizing the potential of marketing to major insurers highlights one pattern that is integral to many successes: Tie your cart to a horse that you know is going to be around for the long run. There have been insurance companies for millennia; they aren't going away. The danger today is to mistake major media attention for a lasting business model.

A recent social media event illustrated this. Social media itself is here to stay, but it's more difficult to say that about any single player. Vine, Twitter's early video offshoot, is an example of that. After a much-celebrated launch, it died a slow death. While it was still alive and kicking, many individuals established themselves as influencers on Vine. When Vine shut down, it was lights off for many careers.

You can use the lessons learned from pivots like these if you find yourself in a situation where you need to adjust your business plan or if you're planning an entirely new venture. These are always interesting cases to study, and I strongly urge you to take note of them so you can begin to see the patterns behind both failures and successes.

CHAPTER 5

The People Edge

"Surround yourself with the best people you can find, delegate authority, and don't interfere as long as the policy you've decided upon is being carried out."

—RONALD REAGAN

Having the right people on board is essential to the success of any organization, and it is imperative for a company creating the One-Percent Edge. It bears repeating that you don't know what you don't know. The wise leader understands this, and that understanding becomes the foundation for building a great team. You've probably heard business experts say great leaders hire people who are smarter than they are.

Many people believe Ronald Reagan was a great president. Whether you agree isn't important for me to make my point. People thought Reagan would fail, but Reagan surrounded himself with some of the best and the brightest minds America had to offer. As a result, he transformed a struggling economy into one with soaring growth, he rebuilt the military, and he restored alliances. He did what many of his critics thought was impossible.

- Do we have the right people on our team to leverage the One-Percent Edge process?
- Are we leveraging the power of diversity?
- Does our team truly understand our company's purpose?
- Are we providing our team with the necessary tools and training to succeed?
- Do we have too many layers of bureaucracy to react in a timely fashion?
- Do our employees maintain a customer-centric focus?
- Are our employees empowered and accountable?
- How are we attracting and retaining team members?

- What is our employment brand communicating? Is that what we want to and should be projecting?
- Do people want to work for our company because of what it stands for or do they just want a job?
- Is our management building trust and respect?
- Do our employees feel as though they can speak freely without fear of retribution?
- Are there unwritten rules of behavior within our organization that are limiting growth?
- Is our team subscribing to our company values?
- Do our employees see the big picture?
- Do we give our employees an opportunity to craft future strategy and direction?

No one has all the answers, especially in this rapidly changing world. That makes people the most important component to your success.

What skills and people do you need to make your vision for growth a reality? Starting with a clear understanding of your business needs is an important element in developing a company that can leverage the One-Percent Edge.

Cut the Dead Weight

I think this is the hardest piece of the process for business leaders at every level. However, if someone isn't a right fit for the direction your company is headed, then it's time to cut the cord. Even the largest companies have limited budgets to carry team members who aren't on board, who don't have the right skills, or who aren't fully engaged. The Gallup State of the American Workplace survey in February 2017 found that 70 percent of U.S. workers say they feel completely disengaged from their workplace. These employees are emotionally disconnected from their companies and may actually be working against their employers' interests; they are less productive, more likely to steal from their companies, absent more often, and inclined to negatively influence their coworkers and drive customers away.

Gallup estimates that actively disengaged employees cost the United States $450 billion to $550 billion in lost productivity per year.[1] This is troubling as American business attempts to recover ground lost during the financial crisis and reach prerecession levels of prosperity.

Employees with the attitude of "It's not my job" or "That's good enough" are not the right fit for a business working to create and maintain the One-Percent Edge. Your business needs everyone's energy, enthusiasm, and creativity. "It's not my job" should not enter their vocabulary. And "good enough" is never acceptable.

Seniority Is Dead

If yours is like most businesses, it has team members who have been with your organization for years but are no longer pulling their weight. They aren't interested in change, innovation, or even learning new things. They are complacent and happy just the way things are. You don't feel as though you can let them go, because of their tenure with your organization.

That's not the way to think. The common objection to seniority is that it rewards deadwood. Don't be reluctant to promote someone over a long-term employee if that individual has demonstrated a strong commitment to innovation.

Unwritten Organizational Rules: What Does Your Company Culture Really Say?

"People don't resist change. They resist being changed!"

—PETER SENGE

Each individual in your organization has an integral role to play in successfully implementing the One-Percent Edge process. Every voice needs to be heard, and as a business leader, you need to listen. Without the right people on your team, your ability to create an innovative work environment will be difficult at best.

One of the questions I suggest you consider is whether your team is open to the concept of change. Without the right attitude toward organizational innovation, you'll find yourself spinning your wheels and getting nowhere. Innovation and change do not happen with an edict from above. As a business leader, you need to win the hearts and minds of your team. Yet your company's unwritten culture may seriously impede your ability to move the organization forward.

My father lives in an assisted living facility. When I'm not traveling on business, I try to stop by to see him at least once a day. However, on numerous occasions, I have left the house and headed somewhere else only to "wake up" and find myself on my way to my father's place. It's a habit. My mind goes on autopilot. That's not a huge problem when you're driving somewhere and you can correct your course. But such autopilot thinking is troublesome for an organization trying to create the One-Percent Edge and stay relevant in today's market.

The problem with autopilot thinking and habits is that when it comes to business decision making, it often isn't truly visible. Habits develop over time, and most likely your team isn't even aware they exist. If they are aware of them, they likely don't know where the habits originated, and they might not even be able to articulate precisely what they are, but everyone is cognizant of their existence, and no one feels comfortable breaking the pattern. No matter how much rhetoric is espoused, the status quo will remain intact.

Consider the egregious mistakes made by General Motors managers and executives when they failed to recall millions of GM cars with deadly ignition switches. A report released by the company refers to the "GM nod," whereby managers would attend a meeting, discuss a course of action, and subsequently do nothing. GM CEO Mary Barra described it as serious incompetence and complacency; she said she plans to change it. Can you imagine if this were your business? An action plan is agreed upon and yet no action is taken.

Subsequent to identifying the unwritten internal rules, GM launched a "Speak Up for Safety" campaign to encourage employees to raise safety issues quickly. It goes without saying that in every organization, employees should feel free to speak openly about their concerns, but that's frequently not the case. Why? Because of the invisible company culture that has evolved over time.

Probably one of the best examples of a written company culture that is reflected differently in action is Enron. An introductory statement written by CEO Ken Lay read, "As officers and employees of Enron Corp., its subsidiaries, and its affiliated companies, we are responsible for conducting the business affairs of the companies in accordance with all applicable laws and in a moral and honest manner." Lay went on to indicate that the sixty-four-page Enron Code of Ethics reflected policies approved by the company's board of directors and that the company, which enjoyed a reputation for being fair and honest, was highly respected. Enron's ethics code also specified, "An employee shall not conduct himself or herself in a manner which directly or indirectly would be detrimental to the best interests of the Company or in a manner which would bring to the employee financial gain separately derived as a direct consequence of his or her employment with the Company."[2]

One has to wonder how a company with a clearly articulated code of ethics became overcome with greed and deceit. You know what they say: Actions speak louder than words. In this instance, according to many articles and comments, the top leadership and the company's culture evolved into one that condoned unethical behavior, and in my opinion, may have even encouraged it.

At Enron, employees were pushed to make the numbers and meet quotas. Similarly, employees at Wells Fargo felt so pressured to make their quotas that employees began opening fake bank and credit card accounts. Many news stories reported that managers condoned this do-whatever-it-takes mentality. How far up the management ladder did this fraudulent activity go? The jury is still out on that question, but suffice it to say the CEO resigned. This activity became part of the organizational norms over a number of years, and even though employees may have known it wasn't kosher, because it was accepted behavior, they followed suit.

As a leader in a company incorporating the One-Percent Edge process, it's imperative to develop a team poised for action like a racehorse rearing to break out of the gate. Your entire team needs to have a customer-centric focus and an eye toward new opportunities. However, identifying the unwritten cultural norms that may be impeding your growth is never easy.

Talk to your employees. Ask them about any preconceived attitudes they might have toward the company's business operations. Most likely, employees will feel more comfortable discussing these unwritten rules in small groups with no reporting lines included. This can take a considerable amount of time and commitment depending on how deeply rooted these habits are within your organization. But without going through this exercise, your ability to build an organization with the One-Percent Edge will be limited at best, and you may soon find your company fading into irrelevancy.

Large companies can take a cue from the popular TV show *Undercover Boss*. In each episode, the head of a large company puts on a disguise and works beside line-level employees. These CEOs and founders learn a lot about what really happens on a day-to-day basis in their companies.

While you may not be able to do this yourself, you might tweak the "mystery shopper" idea a bit and employ a "mystery new hire." Be creative and show grace to your employees.

Only Reporting What Leadership Wants to Hear

"Good management consists in showing average people how to do the work of superior people."

—JOHN D. ROCKEFELLER

Children often say what they know their parents want to hear, and the same can be true for members of your team. Could your staff be limiting information from you because they are trying to please you?

Consider what happened at Nokia. The company lost the smartphone battle despite having half of the global market share in 2007. While there are many reasons why Nokia failed, making the same mistake twice probably drove the final nail in its corporate coffin. Company leadership was fine continuing to do the same things that powered its initial success, and that included allowing Nokia phones to be powered by its Symbian OS.

It failed to anticipate how Apple's iPhone and iOS would change the mobile phone landscape. Perhaps Nokia could have recovered from that mistake, but when it allowed its corporate egotism to pooh-pooh Google's Android OS smartphone play, it pretty much sealed its fate.

There's one more observation I want to make that illustrates the danger when leadership wears blinders. Nokia, as you may recall, was still posting fairly strong sales in developing markets during the early iOS and Android days. For some reason, leadership was unable to appreciate the fact that as soon as consumers in those developing markets experienced iOS or Android-powered smart-phones, they would want them too.

Game over for Nokia.

Foster an environment that embraces sharing bad news along with good news. The bad news is actually more important to your decision making process as long as it isn't filtered through rose-colored glasses.

Build Great Teams with an Edge

"A small group of thoughtful people could change the world.
Indeed, it's the only thing that ever has."

—MARGARET MEAD

Now that you're aware how unwritten rules and habits can signifi-cantly detract from your business growth and innovation, one way to combat that is to build great teams. Annual employee perfor-mance reviews are a thing of the past because all they do is support the status quo and complacency. Annual performance reviews are far too dated by the time an employee is measured. And honestly, can you really reflect an entire year of work in a single evaluation? Do you keep notes throughout the year? What sticks best in your memory, the good or the bad? Some experts argue that perfor-mance reviews actually hinder peak performance. Some compa-nies, such as the consulting firm Accenture, are eliminating them completely. Accenture CEO Pierre Nanterme explained they are "too costly" and don't achieve the goal of driving better performance.[3]

In addition to shedding the performance review process, more and more companies are eliminating the outdated ranking system that causes intense competitiveness among coworkers. In my first corporate job, you could tell the rank of someone by the size of her cubicle, the number of chairs in her office, and whether she had access to an administrative assistant. In those days, these were the trappings of success.

Rather than complex organizational charts with solid reporting structures, companies are harnessing the power of teams. I'm sure you've heard of situations where the whole is greater than the sum of the parts. That appears to be true with the collective intelligence of teams. Research shows that teams provide increased efficiency, more flexibility, and greater creativity and innovation than individuals working alone. A project conducted by Google discovered that teams see mistakes more quickly and find better solutions to problems. It has also been reported that people working in teams tend to achieve better results and report higher job satisfaction, which of course enhances profitability.

There is a caveat, however: While performance reviews, as we know them, are disappearing, measuring performance completely is not. Business leaders in highly functional companies today are providing real-time feedback to employees. Regular one-on-one meetings allow for the setting of priorities, a discussion of achievement, and some coaching and development. Additionally, peer performance review is scheduled regularly in an open environment. While some team members may be reluctant to participate, strong business leaders train employees for those hard conversations by explaining their importance to the company's growth.

Why are some teams successful while others are not? Google created Project Aristotle to research what makes the best teams and learn how to put them together. In many respects, it was like herding cats. The researchers couldn't find any clear patterns. They looked at research by psychologists and sociologists on group norms—the unwritten rules that govern group behavior—and then the challenge became how to influence group norms.

A study conducted by Carnegie Mellon University, the Massachusetts Institute of Technology, and Union College found that the thing that distinguished good groups from dysfunctional ones was how the teammates treated one another. The right norms could raise the group's collective intelligence, whereas the wrong norms would hobble a team even if individually all the members were exceptionally bright. All got an equal amount of time to speak. "As long as everyone got a chance to talk, the team did well," said lead researcher Anita Williams Woolley. "But if only one person or a small group spoke all the time, the collective intelligence declined."[4]

Good groups also have high average social sensitivity; they are intuitive at discerning how others feel based on tone of voice, expressions, and nonverbal cues. They are sensitive to one another's moods and share personal stories and emotions. Members of these kinds of teams feel safe to express opinions and take risks.

This may be the biggest insight researchers have found. If you want to leverage the power of teams, your employees must feel psychologically safe. Coworkers need to invest the time to create mutual bonds and a sense of interpersonal safety.

Team Building Blocks

People need to know how their work fits into the larger mission. Playing a small role in an important production is fine, but playing a small role in a pointless production is toxic for teamwork and productivity.

Keep tabs on team effectiveness. Measure how long it takes between the time team members discover a problem and when they decide to say something about it. The longer time it takes, the more dysfunction creeps into the group. Morale drops and members become unengaged. The gossip mill grows rampant, and miscommunication begins to take over. Create an environment where people feel comfortable to bring up issues in a timely fashion.

Build diversity into your teams. A *Harvard Business Review* article notes a body of recent research finding that nonhomogenous teams are smarter.[5] When you work with people who are different from you, you're challenged to think in different ways. You shed your stale ways of thinking and are pushed out of the autopilot habits that have limited performance. We're always talking about thinking out of the box; it's impossible to do if everyone at the table thinks alike.

Need more persuasion? Consider these findings:

► In a study published in *Innovation: Management, Policy & Practice*, the authors analyzed levels of gender diversity in research and development teams from 4,277 companies in Spain. They found that companies with more women were more likely to introduce radical new innovations into the market over a two-year period. Other studies have found that cultural diversity enhances innovation.[6]

► A 2015 McKinsey report on 366 public companies found those in the top quartile for ethnic and racial diversity in management were 35 percent more likely to have financial returns above their industry mean, and those in the top quartile for gender diversity were 15 percent more likely to have returns above the industry mean.[7]

► A *Harvard Business Review* article notes that diverse teams are more likely to examine facts more closely; and diverse panels raise more fact-related questions and make fewer factual errors.[8]

Working with people who look just like you may feel more comfortable, but you shouldn't be lulled into a false sense of security. Conformity, groupthink, habits, and unwritten rules kill innovation and prevent the development of the One-Percent Edge.

One for All and All for One

Frequently, organizations find themselves in competition internally. Departments compete for resources, and the left hand doesn't know what the right hand is doing. Redundancy occurs. Customer service, both internally and externally, suffers. And innovation dies because there is no common vision. Each group is competing for its "win" with no regard to the overall organization. They have created their own little kingdoms.

Behavioral science experts agree that competition per se isn't necessarily bad. Think about the generation of children who have gotten trophies just for showing up. As Pittsburgh Steelers linebacker James Harrison said, "Sometimes your best is not enough and that should drive you to want to do better."[9] So competition is healthy to a degree, and it's important to reward those who excel. But when the competition becomes so fierce within your organization that collaboration is impossible, then it's your job to tear down the walls.

Regardless of the nature of your business, your company needs to be agile in order to create a competitive edge. A successful organization is completely aligned in terms of strategy, goals, and vision. Alignment keeps the organization moving in the right direction with all the players understanding the direction.

To prevent internal strife from derailing your quest for innovation and relevance, make sure you're communicating that the whole is greater than the sum of its parts. Consider rewarding employees based on how well they work together. Make sure they are aware of how other departments, groups, and teams impact the company's goals. One company I consulted had a designated member from other departments attend staff meetings to learn what the department was working on and report back.

Keep in mind that the real competitors are the external forces that are putting your business at risk. Redirect the focus to the external and make it a company-wide challenge to defeat the external competition.

The Mark of an Employee with the One-Percent Edge

Many business leaders recognize the importance of good team members. But how do you identify an employee who is well suited to help you build a culture that can achieve the One-Percent Edge? While there's no checklist, here are three intangible qualities you can look for:

▶ **Team player.** I've mentioned this before, but the words "It's not my job" are as irritating to me as fingernails on a chalkboard. A team member with the edge isn't worried about her job description. She sees the big picture and eagerly does whatever needs to be done to ensure success.

▶ **Out-loud thinker.** As I noted in Chapter 2, "The Leadership Edge," you must create an environment in which your team feels comfortable to speak up. But even in the most open work environments there will be individuals who simply won't speak out. An employee with the edge doesn't hold back. He will question decisions and point out problems immediately.

▶ **Restless.** Employees with the edge are never truly satisfied. Complacency is an enemy. They are always tinkering with better ways to do things and thus help to continually enhance your overall business strategy. These individuals are entrepreneurial thinkers.

Investing in People: Hire for Life

You can't build great teams if you don't make the right hiring choices from the beginning. Having the wrong people on your team comes at a significant cost. The money you spend hiring team members is your LAC—labor acquisition cost. Your LAC can range from hundreds to thousands of dollars. A high turnover in personnel can result in significant costs that can cripple your business—not to mention other costs such as lost opportunities, productivity, and morale.

Every task someone in your workforce completes generates revenue for your company. The goal is that the per-task revenue generates gross profit that goes back into your company. However, with rapid turnover, your gross profit may never cover the LAC. When you hire someone, it's like going into debt. You have to pay back the debt (or, in this case, the LAC) before you make money. If the employee quits or is terminated before that debt is paid off, then you lose money. The bigger your company gets, the greater this cost can add up.

Solution? Make the right hires, and give them a reason to stay. Provide incentives for them to work hard and contribute to the company's vision. Make employee satisfaction one of the key factors you measure in your business. Companies with the One-Percent Edge hire for the long term, not just for an open position. They want someone who will perform well over time.

My cousin worked part time for Chick-fil-A during high school, and she couldn't say enough good things about her work environment. The company has done an exceptional job of creating a consistent and strong customer service focus. Instead of training people to be pleasant and say *please* and *thank you*, the company hires people who already understand the virtue of politeness. The company's store-operator turnover rate is only 5 percent. Casual dining restaurants average a 44 percent turnover rate, according to a report in *Nation's Restaurant News*.[10]

In his book, *Four Seasons: The Story of a Business Philosophy*, Four Seasons CEO Isadore Sharp writes, "I can teach anyone to be a waiter, but you can't change an ingrained poor attitude."[11]

Cure the Hiring Headache

There's a commercial for an online recruiting and hiring service that features people complaining about the large amount of time they spend sorting through résumés before they started using the online service.

I don't know if the company featured in this commercial is any good, but I do know that recruiting talent and bringing the right people on board can be extremely time consuming, and the results aren't always the best. And if you follow business surveys, you'll know that the shortage of excellent candidates is perennially cited as one of the biggest problems facing business owners.

This is often a problem for one simple reason: timing. There is no guarantee that the best talent will be available when you start to recruit for an open position.

To solve this dilemma, consider changing your approach to recruiting and adopt a long-range view: Recruit for talent more than for open positions.

If you are deeply involved in your industry or in your community, you probably have a good feel for who are the all-stars or potential all-stars. Establish relationships with these people and try to bring them onto your team even when you don't have a specific position you want to fill. Leaders of the best companies will sometimes create positions for individuals who they believe would be instrumental in helping move their companies forward. This is especially true when you're planning for growth. It takes motivated, talented, and experienced professionals to successfully pilot growth initiatives.

When these individuals pop up on your radar screen, respect them and what they bring to the table. Don't allow a bureaucratic HR system to cost you a great team member. Don't make an experienced and desirable candidate jump through a lot of unnecessary hoops.

I mentioned the importance of establishing relationships with the top talent. Work hard to maintain and even improve on that relationship as you are going through the hiring process. Be sure that the person has the chance to start building relationships with department leaders and future coworkers.

Realize that if you're working with a great candidate who is willing to change companies, there's a good chance you aren't the only company expressing interest in the professional. If the phone line goes dead at any point in the recruiting-hiring process, the candidate may assume that you've lost interest.

Why People Quit

We've talked about getting great people in through the front door, but if you want to hire for life, you also have to prevent them from going out the back door.

When people quit, the reason they most often cite is that they have had a problem with management, usually with their direct supervisor. This puts a premium on the people who are able to do a good job supervising others.

Unfortunately, many leaders think that because a person has demonstrated excellent performance for one job within the company, that person will take the same level of excellence into a supervisory or management role. That's not always true.

Have you noticed how few Hall of Fame baseball players end up as managers after their careers are over?

In the same way, if you look at the managers who have made it to the Hall of Fame, you rarely find any of the game's biggest names. A recent managerial inductee is Tony La Russa, who I enjoyed following for years as he guided the St. Louis Cardinals through many championship seasons.

However, as an infielder in the major leagues, La Russa's lifetime batting average was mediocre: .199.

The problem with great players is that they can't relate to the average players. They expect everyone to live up to their standards. The same problem can pop up when you're selecting managers for your business. Also, different business situations require different managerial strengths.

Let's look at some attributes that will help you determine who on your staff should do well when promoted to manager:

▶ **Leadership skills.** All managers should have some leadership skills. But in some environments, it should be one of the manager's strongest skills. If you're in a turnaround situation, opening a new area of business, or are experiencing difficulties in one department, strong leadership is required.

▶ **Organizational skills.** Good organizational skills will be needed at times in any managerial position, but sometimes they are critical. If you sense that efficiency is suffering, you need to bring in a manager who can see past the clutter and get the machine running smoothly.

▶ **Ability to control.** Are personnel issues holding back your company? Leadership and organization are required, but the ability to maintain control is highlighted. To keep control, you need someone who can have frank conversations with employees without losing her cool, which brings us to the next quality.

▶ **Proper temperament.** Anger has no place in management, although almost everyone suffers the occasional bout. Sometimes star employees are also the most passionate employees. They can have a difficult time controlling their emotions. If you're planning to promote such an individual, before you make the move, have a long talk about temperament and make sure the person knows your expectations. Also, be prepared to work on this area with employees who you feel would otherwise do a good job in management.

▶ **Communication skills.** Excellent communication skills are a hallmark of most great managers. If you're in a technical industry, your most skilled techie may be your best employee. However, this person may have poor communication skills—and no desire to develop them. Don't promote your tech wizard just because he has been so valuable as an employee.

▶ **Teaching nature.** Along the small-business growth curve, there are times when you want to replicate certain people. If you have a star employee who has a natural ability to teach others, this person could make a good manager. On the flip side, there are people who like to keep their special knowledge to themselves to maintain their superiority. Watch out for them, even if they excel at their jobs.

Choosing the right individuals for promotion is as much an art as a science. Keep these qualities in mind and try to avoid a real-life demonstration of the Peter Principle: promoting people to the level of their incompetence.

When you have Hall of Fame employees, you can find other ways to advance their careers without pulling them into management. You can give them special projects and additional responsibilities that expand your business and take advantage of their special talents and energy. This will keep them on board for the long run.

A company with the One-Percent Edge builds teams of leaders not managers, mentors instead of performance reviewers. They nurture people to be the best they can be and encourage and prepare them to take on challenges and increased responsibility. They give their team members the opportunity to flourish and prosper.

The Circle of Trust

In Chapter 2, "The Leadership Edge," I talked about the importance of trust, integrity, and authenticity of leadership. Now that we are talking about building your team, let's discuss how to build core trust with your team members.

It should come as no surprise to you that in an organization where employees feel genuinely cared about, employees are more engaged. There is an emotional connection that binds them to the company and that correlates to how motivated and empowered they feel.

In the comedy film *Meet the Parents*, Robert De Niro's character tells his future son-in-law, played by Ben Stiller, that his family has a circle of trust and Stiller shouldn't violate that trust. In the movie, De Niro plays an intimidating figure, but it does make a salient point about the importance of trust in any relationship. Organizational experts for many years have known that employees in high-trust organizations are more productive, have more energy at work, collaborate better, and stay with their employers longer. In a 2016 global CEO survey, PwC found more than half of CEOs think that a lack of trust is a threat to their organization's growth.[12]

Trust runs two ways. In addition to your team trusting you as a leader, you must in turn trust your team. You can't develop true loyalty by simply telling your team you trust them. You need to back it up with action. They need to know you have their backs and if they start to fall, you'll be there to catch them.

Building Trust Within Your Organization

Here are some guidelines for building two-way trust in an organization that wants to achieve the One-Percent Edge:

▶ **Don't compromise your values.** You set the moral tone in your business. Don't let your moral values slide. If you do, it's a clear signal to your team that they can cut corners and not have to worry about their integrity. Going back to my Chick-fil-A example, the restaurants close on Sunday because of the owners' religious beliefs. The same is true for Goedeker's Appliances in St. Louis. In television commercials, the appliance store-owner says they are open every day from 10:00 a.m. to 6:00 p.m., except Sundays they are closed for the Lord's Day. Think about all the business opportunities these companies miss by closing on Sundays. Yet that is at the core of their values, and it can't be compromised.

▶ **Don't be a hypocrite.** Trust is built on relationships where one's actions and words are in harmony with each other. The quickest way to break someone's trust is to say one thing and then turn around and do something else.

▶ **Hire for values and character.** Technical skills can be overrated. Prisons are full of criminals who are proficient technically. You can teach skills. By the time men and women are adults, it's virtually impossible to teach character and values. Every organization needs employees who mesh with its core values because values drive business decisions. Employees who do not adhere to a company's values end up diluting them. It's important to screen your job candidates for a good cultural fit. Tony Hsieh, the CEO of Zappos, said he will fire someone regardless of his job performance if he isn't living up to and subscribing to the Zappos values.[13]

▶ **Be a listener.** You need to hear, understand, and process what your employees are saying before you can make a good reply. Don't talk over people at meetings. Listening is a skill you need to develop. If your team isn't talking to you about issues, that doesn't mean they aren't talking; they could be talking in front of your customers and clients—and undermining your business. Flight attendants are notorious for this type of behavior. They congregate in the galley and share their gripes with one another. Travelers nearby get to listen to their woes instead of getting the service they paid for.

► **Resolve problems.** If there is a problem between you and an employee, or between two employees, don't let it fester. It will only get worse.

► **Don't hold onto anger or grudges.** This is similar to the last point, but with a slight twist. Sometimes things happen in the workplace that merely annoy us, and frankly, sometimes it's our attitudes that allow us to get annoyed in the first place. For a very small infraction, just let it go—completely. Forgive and forget. You also unintentionally rub people the wrong way occasionally, I'm sure.

► **Be honest but not hurtful.** When you need to straighten things out with others on your team, be sure you have clarity when you bring up the subject. There are ways to be honest without inflicting additional pain on the individual. Think about the best approach to take. Don't chastise someone in haste.

► **Understand they have a life.** As you know, the lines between work and our personal lives have blurred. Some of us have adapted to that pace by practically working 24/7, but the same is not true for millennials. A report published by the U.S. Chamber of Commerce Foundation noted that transparency, collaboration, and a seamless work-life balance are not only vital to millennials' comfort but also to their success within the workplace. Many of us spend as much time with our work "families" as we do with our real families—if not more. Trust is critical for success and satisfaction. If you consistently model trust and the behaviors that support trust, it will be returned to you.

Inspire People to Achieve Their Own Greatness

Are you spurring your team members to be the best they can be? Thomas Edison was arguably one of the most brilliant minds in the world, but he knew he didn't have all the answers, so he gave his assistants the opportunity to flourish. He instructed them on the general idea of what he wanted and then encouraged them to work out a solution on their own. In some cases he even refused to help them with their experiments. But he knew that if he selected the right people, together they could achieve great results.

When you hire the right people for your team, you need to get out of their way and let them do their thing. Your business will benefit from the creativity and diversity of ideas.

Employee Recognition Is a Great Motivator

Employees like to feel they are being treated fairly financially, but in this day and age, money isn't the only motivator. That's why there are annual competitions for the "Best Places to Work." Personally, I know many people who say that workplace environment was why they willingly accepted offers for less money than they could have received elsewhere. A highly successful and innovative company needs energized employees who know that hard work—going the extra mile—will be noticed and rewarded. Too often I find that companies fall down on this simple characteristic. Employees feel as though they give, give, give—and management takes it for granted. "They don't pay me enough to put up with his s--t!"

In fact, employees who really feel taken advantage of can easily sabotage your growth. For example, Blue Apron, the home meal kit company, experienced serious workplace issues, including violence among workers. The *New York Post* reported that in fall 2016, three fights broke out during the night shift at the company's New Jersey facility.[14] BuzzFeed reported of violence in the company's West Coast facility, and the California Division of Occupational Safety and Healthy reportedly found unsafe working conditions putting the start-up company's employees at risk for fractured bones, chemical burns, and more.[15] There is speculation that until

Blue Apron's leadership gets this situation under control, the company may have to postpone any attempts for an IPO.

Conversely, Yum Brands has a mission of growing the world's leading restaurant brand, and its employees are behind that initiative 100 percent. The company has a robust recognition program that honors employees for noteworthy achievement. Former CEO David Novak said in a keynote speech at a MUFSO conference, (an event that brings together the restaurant industry's top leaders, innovators, experts and change makers to reveal business insights that are laser focused on moving the restaurant industry forward). "You have to take people with you to make big things happen. You have to get your 'people capability' right to give customers what they're really looking for."[16]

For Novak, who wrote the book *Taking People with You: The Only Way to Make Big Things Happen* (a guide for successful leadership based on the principles he developed during his years at Yum Brands' helm), the recognition program was an integral part of the success equation. His office wall was filled with pictures of smiling team members from all levels. All of the winners not only received the photo opportunity, but they were also awarded cash along with a set of plastic smiling teeth with legs to reflect that they "walk the talk."

Shine the Spotlight

It is likely that you have people on your team right now with hidden talents. Those talents could easily help you identify new ways of doing business. But depending on the size of your organization, it can be difficult to get beyond the functional aspects of someone's job. As a business leader, it's important to discover those hidden treasures, but you are going to have to do a little digging. Once those special skills are uncovered, however, if you can pair them to the right position, you'll have a match made in heaven. Your company will benefit, and the employee will excel.

"Employees who identify their talents and passions and apply those toward driving business usually do much better," said Dan Coughlin, a training consultant who works with companies to get the best performance from workers. "Employers can create a very motivating workplace by asking staff about their strengths and passions."

Boston-based State Street Corporation took an unusual approach to discovering hidden talents: It hosted its own TED event. In case you don't know, TED is the online conference that has taken the country by storm, offering "riveting talks by remarkable people." All talks are less than eighteen minutes and are highly produced. A quick glance at TED's YouTube channel shows its online content has been viewed well over one billion times.

State Street decided to identify its speakers from its own pool of about 30,000 employees. State Street's chief marketing officer, Hannah Grove, who came up with the idea, told *Businessweek* that they had people from all geographies and all levels of the company. Grove came up with the concept to market the company's brand but also to encourage employee bonding and the sharing of ideas. TED's head of global partnerships, Ronda Carnegie said, "It makes you realize corporations are made up of people."

On the day of State Street's TED event, Joe Kowan, a graphic designer at State Street, shared a story about how he got over stage fright by making up a silly song. Sitting in the very front row was State Street's chief executive officer, Jay Hooley. Later, Kowan said, "I felt this overwhelming support from everyone. It leveled the playing field in a way I wasn't expecting."[17]

Why not use this strategy to spark some creativity in your organization? Challenge members of your team to put together eighteen-minute presentations on innovation topics. Keep the parameters as open ended as possible.

Benefits you can expect to achieve:

- Your team will understand that you are truly committed to innovation and independent thinking.

- You will plant the seeds for innovative change in your company.
- You may discover that some of your employees have talents and knowledge you were previously unaware of.

If you don't think your business is big enough to support its own TED event, use TED online resources to your advantage. Scan the most popular online TED Talks to see which hit closest to home for what you're trying to accomplish. Take time from an occasional staff meeting to view and discuss an inspirational or thought-provoking TED Talk.

Training consultant Coughlin, a former athletic coach, borrows a few techniques from the playing field in his approach to business coaching. He suggests huddling with staffers. "Small meetings can give business leaders valuable information about what drives their employees and how those talents can be used to grow the company," he said. Employee outings can also reveal some unique characteristics. Create an environment allowing individuals to showcase their unique abilities. Create an ongoing dialogue about each individual's unique perspectives.

Motivate with Purpose

Innovative organizations need energy, and energy comes from passion and purpose. Yet most companies spend their time focused on profits, shareholders, market share, etc. Employees don't feel energized, because they don't understand the company's purpose. Why do we exist other than to make money? People want to contribute to something bigger than themselves. They want to feel their life and work are meaningful and that they serve a higher purpose, aligned with their highest values.

A number of years ago, I was hired to work with a major brand on a new website portal the company was launching for small and midsize businesses. The internal marketing team had been assigned the task of selling it to this market segment and to quickly ramp up participation. Without understanding the real value they were providing these customers, they created a new initiative and were doing their best to sell it to the market.

I could immediately see that it was a knee-jerk reaction to a mandate without much real consideration for the customer. In my opinion, the portal was of no real benefit to busy organizational leaders, and in fact, it appeared to create even more confusion and work. Yet the marketing team tried diligently to force customers to jump on board.

When results were lackluster, I finally asked the discouraged team, "What purpose are you serving behind the new launch?" They stumbled around with boilerplate language but ultimately admitted they really didn't know why the product was needed in the first place. It was like cramming a square peg into a round hole.

Compare this result to that of Southwest Airlines. Employees there usually seem like they are having fun. They are helpful and they smile at their customers. Why? Because they understand their purpose:

"We exist to connect people to what's important in their lives through friendly, reliable, and low-cost air travel."

—Southwest Airlines purpose statement.

According to Southwest CEO Gary Kelly, "Southwest is a great place to work and brings the greatest joy because we have such meaningful purpose."[18]

Whether you are leading a small company or a big business, your team needs to be evangelists. This means that you need to get their buy in, and to do that they must know the "why" behind your company's decisions. A purpose mobilizes people in a way that pursuing profits alone never will. "Here's the product—now go sell it" won't excite and energize your team. When employees know why they are doing something (other than to make money for the company) and what purpose it serves in the market, it ignites their passion. No longer a task of selling to make quotas, instead it becomes an ability to serve the market. And as you know, when you truly believe in your product, you don't have to sell anything.

The mission statement of your company serves as the broad perspective purpose of your business. But each new initiative must also have a purpose, and it is mandatory that its purpose should be in line with your mission statement.

Culture by Design or Default

Business leaders know about company culture. There is nothing new about this buzzword. Your company culture can be by design or default; unfortunately, far too many companies fall into the default mode. Very few truly understand the process of building a strong company culture. A company culture isn't about having the cool nap rooms or free beverages and snacks. Those things are cosmetic. The bloom of the rose fades fast when leadership styles run afoul of the company's purported values.

A company culture is something that permeates the organization and strengthens as you add people who fit with that culture. According to the 2016 Job Market Report, only 3 in 10 respondents felt like they had made the ultimate culture connection. When your employees don't feel like they click, they become disengaged, unhappy, restless, and less productive. Employee attrition rates are high. In fact, one source found 63 percent of employees were planning a job change.[19] How can you be innovative and agile when your team membership looks like a revolving door? You can't.

A company with the One-Percent Edge has a strong culture. It stands for something. It's a place where people want to work and a place where current members recruit their friends to join them. Yet too frequently, companies focus on profit-and-loss statements and shareholder value, and they completely ignore the culture. Making money isn't a purpose or a motivator. Delivering value to the market is.

The CEO and cofounder of Airbnb, Brian Chesky, wrote a memo to his team about the importance of maintaining the company's culture. After equity investor Peter Thiel invested $150 million of Series C money in the company, Thiel said, "Don't f--k up the culture." The remark caused Chesky to stop and think: How could he ensure the company would get it right?

Then he realized, "Culture is simply a shared way of doing something with passion." He continued by explaining that the company would evolve over the years, but the one thing that should remain the same is the culture. "[C]ulture . . . creates the foundation for all future innovation. If you break the culture, you break the machine that creates your products," he explained.[20]

With the right culture and the right team, your company can move mountains. You can address problems and find creative solutions.

Getting Creativity Rocking with Your Team

Once you have the right players on your team, you want to give them the best opportunity to succeed. That means they need time to think. As I said in Chapter 1, the first step in the One-Percent Edge process is mindful thinking. Think time is critical for innovation. If you have too much on your plate, there is no room for creative ideas.

Intuit gives employees 10 percent of their hours as unstructured time. The legal department created a toolkit that lets product managers try new business ideas without needing to talk to company lawyers. The IT department accelerated the time it took to set up test environments for new web products from two months to two hours.

In order to ensure that its team members have inspiring work, Google provides an allowance for 20 percent free time. This program is responsible for some of the company's most innovative products, including Gmail and Google Suggest.

Unleash the Entrepreneurial Spirit

Regardless of the size of your organization, a company that nurtures an entrepreneurial spirit is going to be on the cutting edge of innovation. When the spark of entrepreneurship gets smothered, the organization begins to stagnate.

It's not easy to create the sense of entrepreneurship or intrapreneurship as your organization grows, but the benefits are significant. Such an environment doesn't just happen. Business leaders must make a commitment to it and take steps to ensure it happens.

One great way is to hire people who aspire to be entrepreneurs and make them feel like partners, not employees. When people take ownership, they feel more responsible for outcomes and achievements.

Google organizes its entire firm to support and cultivate unplanned entrepreneurship and innovation. It accomplishes this with the 20-percent free time policy, open development environments, a flat organizational structure, and recognition and rewards for successful innovation. The result of this entrepreneurial environment has been increased productivity and innovation for the company.

3M has long given its engineers the freedom to take 15 percent of their time to work on any idea that comes to mind. Whenever you use a Post-it note, you're enjoying the fruit of that philosophy.

CHAPTER 6

The Marketing Edge

"Stop racing after every new fad and focus on making consistent, emotional connections with consumers. If you stand for nothing, you fall for everything."

—KEVIN ROBERTS

N ow it's time to apply the One-Percent Edge process to ensure your marketing messages remain relevant to your customers. To do that, you'll need to get away from your office to where your customers and clients are. It need not be a physical presence; it can be a virtual one. But you do need to hear what your customers are saying. What types of messages resonate with them? How can you cut through the competition clutter to reach them?

- How can we cut through the information clutter?
- How can we truly connect with our customers?
- Do our marketing messages resonate with our target customers?
- How can we create integrated experiences?
- How can we engage people to become customers for life?
- How are we making the world a better place?
- What do we believe in? What do we stand for? What's our brand promise?
- What is our perceived value? Are there better ways to communicate it?
- How can customers become brand evangelists for our company?
- Are we listening to the voice of the customer to understand what customers need?
- Is there a gap between our brand promise and what we're delivering to customers?
- What opportunities exist to drive growth through changes in marketing and sales strategies?

Think and Reflect

A big mistake companies make is to guess about what will work or won't work with their target markets. You may think you know your customers, but in reality you only know who they were yesterday. And you might be surprised to know what they're really thinking about your company.

Brand Promise

The foundation of your brand is your purpose—why you're in business. It doesn't say what you do but rather what you promise the market. It's your value proposition. The message is communicated through the strategic execution of your marketing strategies. You want to make an emotional connection with your market.

As much as we like to think we make logical decisions, we are largely driven by our emotions. Clinical psychologist and psychoanalyst Mary Lamia, Ph.D., wrote an article for *Psychology Today* titled "Like It or Not, Emotions Will Drive the Decisions You Make Today."[1]

This is why we spend so much time emphasizing the importance of building relationships with prospects, customers, and clients. It's not that logic and reasoning play no role in purchase decisions, but there has to be an emotional trigger and/or emotional foundation for the commercial relationship to flourish.

I also think that these emotional connections will be even more important in the coming years. Millennials, for example, have been found to generally prefer experiences to things. Have you ever watched any of the *Tiny House* shows on HGTV? *Tiny House Hunters, Tiny House Living,* and the others are about people who build, buy, and live in, well, tiny houses. They are almost exclusively millennials, and the primary reason they give for choosing a tiny house is that they would rather spend their money on funding experiences, such as travel, than a larger home.

If you fail to make these experiential, emotional connections, you'll find your company constantly competing for business and being threatened by competition.

For you to maintain relevancy with your market, your customers need to know the value you provide and how it benefits them. Your brand needs to touch your customers in a personal and intimate way. If you see your business as a business of margins, then you are coming close to being a commodity.

Many companies use their brand promise as a tagline. Here are a few of my favorites.

- BMW: "The Ultimate Driving Machine."
- Apple: "Think Different." Although it's debatable whether it is grammatically correct, it conveys the fact that Apple products are not the same old same old.
- Geico: "15 minutes can save you 15% or more on car insurance." This simple concept has propelled Geico to the top of its industry. Well, the cute little gecko is pretty memorable too.

Your brand promise should communicate what you stand for, and you should commit to making sure you deliver on it. Gallup research found that brands only deliver on their brand promise half the time. However, the highest-performing companies in Gallup's database deliver on their brand promise 75 percent of the time, according to their customers. These companies have greater levels of customer engagement, which enable them to surpass their competitors in terms of share of wallet, profitability, revenue, and relationship growth.

You are competing for attention in the marketplace. Once you get your customer's attention, you've got to show you deserve to keep it.

The key to building a strong brand is to pay attention to your customers. They are better informed, more critical, less loyal, and harder to read than ever before.

No matter what your business is, people don't make decisions based on facts alone; they make them on emotions, feelings. But the most customers (62 percent in fact) don't feel or behave this way. They're indifferent or actively disengaged, which means they're open to switching brands. Companies that can create strong brand promises and consistently deliver on them have a legitimate opportunity to sway these customers and gain a greater share of the market.

In order to remain relevant and build on their success, brands must connect with and engage their customers and tap into their emotions. You want people to trust your brand, to feel good about it. You want customers and clients to have a profound sense of attachment. You want them to fall in love with your brand. Here's how:

- Deliver what you say you will and then some.
- Continually innovate and strive for enhancements.
- Make every contact first class and easily facilitated.
- Always be authentic and accountable.
- Protect your reputation and maintain your integrity at all times.
- Understand that perception of value is critical.
- Convey your uniqueness.
- Empower employees to follow through.

Apple is a brand with extremely loyal customers. Even when Apple messes up, its customers are forgiving. Why? Because it has done what many brands can't—create an emotional connection with its customers. That's why people line up outside Apple stores to purchase the newest product. And think about this: In the height of the Great Recession, shopping malls were nearly empty, except for the Apple store. There, people lined up to make purchases, and they weren't buying trinkets. People love the brand and are willing to pay a higher price for its perceived value.

The same is true for Starbucks. In New York City, there is a Starbucks on almost every block, and they are usually packed with customers even though other brands are just as good or better—and cost less. (Personally, I'm a fan of Dunkin' Donuts.) In a blind taste test conducted by *Consumer Reports* in 2007, McDonald's coffee beat both Starbucks and Dunkin' Donuts.[2] Starbucks doesn't have raving fans, it has fanatical fans. In fact, both Starbucks and Apple have created almost cultlike followings. It's not always just the product; it's the entire experience and sense of community.

When you differentiate your product and you understand how it speaks to your customer, you are building perceived value. Customers will pay a higher price for what they value.

The Brand Promise Gap

"If a good brand is a promise, then a great brand is a promise kept."

—**MUHTAR KENT**, president, Coca-Cola Company

Articulating your brand promise is only the first step in the process. Your company needs to deliver on that promise consistently. That means everyone in your organization must be on board and understand how a failure to live up to the brand promise leaves customers frustrated and reflects poorly on your business. Gallup's research revealed only 27 percent of employees strongly agree that they always deliver on the promises they make to their customers.[3]

A study by management consultant Bain & Company found that 80 percent of business leaders believe their firm offers a superior proposition. However, only 8 percent of customers held that same view.[4] To create the One-Percent Edge, you must do an extensive audit of your company to determine whether your customers understand, believe, and trust your brand promise. Don't assume anything. As I previously mentioned, you may think you know your customer, but the reality may be just the opposite.

Typically, marketing departments and agencies create the brand promise and then incorporate it into slick marketing campaigns. That sets customer expectations. However, most companies admit that when it comes to making operational decisions, they do not take into account the brand promise. And that is the culprit that creates the gap.

Consider RadioShack's brand promise: "You've got questions. We've got answers." You may recall from the introduction, Radio-Shack abandoned its core customer as it chased revenue and fads. So by the time the company unleashed this brand promise, the in-store clerks were ill equipped to be helpful.

Contrast that to Ace Hardware's brand promise: "Being the most helpful hardware stores on the planet." From an operational standpoint, Ace makes sure its in-store associates are well trained to deliver on that promise. It's not enough to talk about your brand promise; you have to support it operationally.

"The goal of a brand promise for a company—and its customers—is really one and the same," said John Surane, Executive Vice President of marketing, merchandising, and sales for Ace Hardware Corporation. "It's a contract the brand is making with their customers about what kind of experience customers can expect when interacting with the brand."[5]

When I was teaching an M.B.A. course on growth strategies for entrepreneurs, my friend, customer-service guru and best-selling author, Shep Hyken, agreed to speak to my students. Shep had recently released his book *Amaze Every Customer Every Time*, in which he cites Ace Hardware's ability to deliver on its brand promise. One of my students then related a story about how some friends and he went to an Ace Hardware one night to buy materials to build a bong. An older woman who was working in the store offered her assistance. They told her what they wanted, but assumed she would be of no help at all. Instead, she walked them through the store and helped them get everything they needed, delivering on the brand promise.

Keep in mind you can offer the best products/services in the world, but if your customer doesn't perceive it that way or trust you because of broken promises, your company will suffer.

The Customer's Voice

"Your customers are not loyal. The brutal truth is that 75 percent of your customers would gladly do business with the competition—because companies have not created the emotional connection that creates customer loyalty and advocacy."

—Leadership expert BILL HOGG

That's why you need to make sure you have a reliable way to hear your customer's voice.

According to research published on CMO.com, 95 percent of companies say they regularly listen to their customers. Of these, 84 percent regularly ask customers for feedback, while 11 percent do so occasionally. Yet despite this widespread collection of customer feedback, only 29 percent of firms with a voice-of-the-customer (VoC) program in place systematically incorporate insights about customer needs into their decision making processes. And nearly three-fourths don't think that their VoC programs are effective at driving actions.[6] What good is data if you're not going to analyze it and use it? When a customer takes time to provide feedback and no action is taken, it damages the relationship. Your customers will be less likely to trust you in the future.

Let me take a step back and explain what a VoC program is. Here is the definition from the Six Sigma dictionary:

"The 'voice of the customer' is a process used to capture the requirements/feedback from the customer (internal or external) to provide the customers with the best-in-class service/product quality. This process is all about being proactive and constantly innovative to capture the changing requirements of the customers with time"[7]

No one becomes an industry leader without listening to the customer. When you're competing in today's marketplace, the playing field is the customer experience and the prize is customer loyalty. An Aberdeen Group report, *The Business Value of Building a Best-in-Class VoC Program*, found companies that have a strong VoC program enjoy a 55 percent customer retention rate.[8] How does that compare with your business?

Intuit has a "We want to hear from you" page on its website. The software giant wants its customers to provide feedback so it can make product enhancements. The company will send a representative to your location, you can meet up with someone at an Intuit location, or you can discuss your idea remotely. To encourage this feedback, Intuit offers customers $75–$150 in Visa gift cards or Intuit software to thank them for their time in helping the company improve its product offerings.

Your company doesn't have to be a large enterprise to develop a VoC program. But what every business needs to succeed is a commitment to the program and a champion to ensure it is executed.

There are ways you can track your customers' behaviors and needs much more effectively so you can create experiences that are more personal and customized. Furthermore, you can do a much better job of predicting future behavior. I'll go into more depth on the technology behind this in Chapter 7, "The Process Edge." But for now, suffice it to say that data collection is at your fingertips via social media analytics, customer relations management software, and website traffic analytics. Consider this your own big data because of what it can do for your business.

The voice of your customers should be in the forefront of your thinking as you create marketing campaigns and search for a message that will be relevant to them. The role of marketing and the chief marketing officer is to "represent customer needs in the business and turn that into commercial opportunity," said Mark Evans, Direct Line Group's marketing director. To do that, he said, "You need to find out what consumers want, challenge the business to deliver that, and tell consumers they can have it."[9]

Social Listening

In Chapter 3, "The Customer Edge," I discussed the importance of using social media to identify and resolve customer concerns. But social media is also a good tool to get a better sense of what the market is saying about your company, product, and services. By monitoring social media platforms, you can measure whether you are living up to your brand promise based on your customers' perceptions. You can also determine whether your marketing messages are resonating with your audience.

What are your customers' pain points? What do they love about your product or service? What are those in your industry talking about? What's being said about your competitors? All of these questions can be answered through the art of social media listening.

Here are some of the things you should follow:

- Your own brand's name (including misspellings)
- Your competitors (again, including misspellings)
- Industry buzzwords
- Brand slogans
- Your CEO or public representatives' names (and misspellings)
- Campaign names or keywords

There are myriad tools to help you track conversations and mentions. Personally, I use Hootsuite and TweetDeck. Quora is a resource that allows you to monitor pertinent questions and discussions. Google Alerts and TalkWalker email you when there are mentions of keywords you're following.

Social listening is also a good tool for marketers to provide an unexpected positive customer experience. For example, a friend was traveling to the wine country in California for a long weekend retreat. She tweeted that she couldn't wait to get to the hotel and schedule her spa services. The hotel's social media manager immediately responded with an offer to schedule her spa services for her in advance. She was blown away.

A few years ago, Staples conducted a fun survey in which small businesses were asked which was more important: 2 million Facebook likes, 2 million Twitter followers, a Super Bowl ad, or a Beyonce endorsement deal. The preference was Facebook. The study also showed that consumer engagement was the primary reason that 50 percent of small business owners used social media.[10]

The Right Marketing Message: Understand the Market Mindset

People want to do business with brands they feel connected to. For brands, that means communicating with consumers in such a way that they can "hear" the message and understand the value of your product.

I'm sure you're familiar with Febreze: Odors out. Freshness in. You've probably seen the television advertisements showing messy, smelly situations where Febreze is sprayed, and then blindfolded and unsuspecting people are ushered into the room. When asked what they smell, they say tropical breezes or flowers. When the blindfold comes off, they are shocked.

Well, not everything has always been so easy for the brand that was introduced in the mid-1990s. When the product launched, the company bought television ads spotlighting how it could eliminate odors. People were seen spraying clothing and furniture to remove pet odors and cigarette smells. P&G thought it was going to be a huge success, but instead it was a big flop. Apparently potential customers didn't want to think they needed the product because that would mean admitting to themselves their homes stunk.

So it was back to the drawing board to see if P&G could figure out a way to get people to buy Febreze. After interviewing (and listening to) customers, the marketing team realized it needed to promote the product as something that comes at the end of cleaning—just a little something extra. A little more perfume content was added to the product to give it a distinct smell, and they redid the campaign. Febreze, the ads implied, was a pleasant finish, not a reminder that your home stinks. Subsequently, sales soared.

To Get People Talking, You Need Brand Ambassadors

One of the best ways to get business has always been through word of mouth. Having recently built a new home in Florida, I'm constantly asking friends and neighbors for home-service-type recommendations. An electrician. A landscaper. A housekeeper, etc. I feel more comfortable relying on their experiences than striking out on my own to find a resource. And I'm not alone. Eighty-four percent of consumers say they either completely or somewhat trust recommendations from family, colleagues, and friends about products and services, making these recommendations the highest ranked source for trustworthiness. And the same holds true in the B2B space: 91 percent of B2B buyers are influenced by word of mouth when making their buying decision.[11]

The importance of word of mouth will only grow in the future because of social platforms. It's easy for your customers and clients to spread the word about your business to thousands of people. To maintain relevance, your business needs to have a laserlike focus on this space. Referrals, comments, and recommendations from actual clients are more credible than anything you can say about your company, as long as the word of mouth is authentic. You can encourage people to share with their followers, but don't put words in their mouths. Likewise, you can't compensate or reward them in any way for a mention without disclosing something has been given in return.

For example, if I write a blog post that is sponsored by a brand, I have to disclose that information on the post itself. And if I post links to the content via social media, I'm required to identify my content as "#sponsored" or "#ad."

Think about what you want your customers to say about your company. In an ideal world, what experience do you want them to share? With that in mind, make sure your marketing messages and strategies are positioned accordingly. And of course, make sure you deliver.

Just as word of mouth via social media and review sites can attract business, it can also drive business away. Sometimes there will be an unhappy and dissatisfied customer who uses a public platform to vent. It happens. Personally, if I see a scathing review that stands out as an aberration from the norm, I ignore it. Chalk it up do someone having a bad day. But too many negative comments can tarnish your brand and affect your ability to grow.

That's why your attention to word of mouth at all levels is an integral part of building a company with the One-Percent Edge. Monitoring online and offline feedback can give you insight into what is working and what isn't. If a bad comment pops up on your Facebook page, address it immediately.

Interestingly, some brands manage this process well and others don't. I had a terrible time booking a reservation for a time-share property I own in Puerto Vallarta. Out of frustration, I posted a lengthy comment on the company's Facebook page. Within ten minutes, customer service was on the phone with me trying to resolve the problem. That kind of response demonstrates the commitment to customers and builds confidence in with your audience.

Lassoing Word of Mouth in the Internet Age

Relying on word-of-mouth advertising is a bit of a gamble. You can do everything right on your end, but you can't force the good word about your business to spread. However, that doesn't mean you're powerless to put to work the positive things people say or think about you. You can use them to create social proof.

Social proof is essentially customer testimony pushed into the Internet age. There should be a prominent place on your company's homepage where you quote good things that customers have said about your product or service. Studies show that these areas are some of the most-read parts of a webpage.

Be sure to include specific details about the person who is saying the good things about your company. Ask for permission, of course, and use her full name and other important identifying details. If your company is business-to-business, include the name of the company the person represents. If you are business-to-consumer, be sure you let readers know exactly what product or service the person used.

Including a headshot is a great idea; it makes the person more "real" to your website visitors.

Also, you may want to create a video of testimonials. Videos are becoming the preferred medium for many website visitors today, and I'm sure that trend will continue to strengthen.

There are a variety of ways you can get social proof on your website. One of the simplest is to ask for it. You know who your best and most satisfied customers are. Ask them if they would contribute a few kind words about your company. Make it easy for them. If they don't have time to create something from scratch, offer to write something for them and submit it for their editing or approval.

If there are online reviews of your product or service—either on your site or on a review site—you can grab quotes from these. The authors have already made their comments public. Be sure to keep them short and cite the source where you found the comments.

Honesty is critical for all of these approaches. Compensating for comments is unethical and can cause you legal problems. If you compensate someone in any way, that fact must be clearly stated in the same location where you use the customer's testimony. If Widget Inc. gives a prospect a free widget to try out and then review, that needs to be declared.

New Marketing Platforms: More Influence Than Traditional Methods

Traditional media may not be dead yet, but their influence on buying decisions is waning. Companies today need to be as innovative about their marketing initiatives as they are about other aspects of their business.

When Floyd Mayweather fought Manny Pacquiao in Las Vegas some years ago, the pay-for-view event was to air commercial free, but that didn't stop Burger King from identifying a unique opportunity to get in front of the audience of 4.4 million. King, Burger King's robed mascot, walked out into the arena next to Mayweather. Experts estimated that Burger King paid Mayweather about $1 million for the opportunity. Innovative marketing such as this has translated into higher restaurant sales.

"Burger King has really found a way to get attention by doing the unexpected and somewhat irreverent," explained Tim Calkins, a marketing professor at Northwestern University's Kellogg School of Management. "They're generating an enormous amount of publicity at a very modest cost."[12]

The good news for small and midsize business is the nontraditional marketing initiatives are less expensive than traditional methods, yet they can be substantially more effective.

Content in Context

When I ran my video-based Internet company, we were ahead of the curve, but we recognized that content on the web would be king. Today, if brands aren't seizing the opportunity to reach the market via this vehicle, they are truly losing out. Eighty-eight percent of B2B marketers use content marketing, allocating 28 percent of their marketing budget to it, according to the Content Marketing Institute. Among consumer-facing marketers, the figures are 76 percent and 32 percent.[13]

Brands that are using content marketing effectively have a written strategy, have a means to evaluate the success of campaigns, and meet regularly to review. Platforms to distribute your content are numerous. A cleverly crafted content program will undoubtedly create an edge for your business. It should be an integral part of your marketing mix as well.

Set yourself apart from the pack by producing content that truly connects with and engages your audience. To build your campaign, start by determining what you want to achieve. Are you trying to attract more visitors to your website? Are you trying to build your community or database? Are you trying to create more brand buzz and awareness?

Next, put yourself in your customers' shoes. What type of content would be helpful and interesting to them? Where do they spend their time online? How do they consume most of their online content? Keep in mind that everyone has a preferred way of consuming information. Some of us like to read. Others prefer visuals such as graphics and video. Finally, some of your customers may be more interested in audio podcasts. You should get a sense of these preferences before you begin.

Take inventory of content you have already produced. I never use a piece of content only once. That's my mantra. If your company has a blog, turn the content into a podcast or video. Then share it around the web. Connect with influencers in your market and build relationships. Then see if they begin to share your content. Also, look for guest-posting opportunities on other websites.

Use analytic tools to identify what's working and what isn't. Google Analytics and insights available on social media platforms will give you a good indication of which content resonates with your audience.

Create your own media house with a branded YouTube channel. Use the channel to showcase your products, provide instructions, explain benefits, and feature customers.

A couple of years ago, I worked on a program with AT&T called the *3:00 Inspiration Break*. We produced short vignettes about business owners and their tips for success. You can still find them on YouTube. The goal of the miniprograms was to give business owners a midafternoon break and a brief bit of inspiration. AT&T wasn't selling its products or services, but the content resonated with important market segments.

Promote your content every opportunity you can. Put links to your social media and content channels on your website, in your newsletters, and in your email signatures.

More and more brands are creating their own content channels to engage with customers and stay relevant to their needs. Farmers Insurance, for example, has a dedicated area to help educate its customers about a variety of topics, including identity theft and how to maintain your house and car. In doing so, Farmers establishes itself as the go-to expert resource, which builds credibility and trust.

Similarly, AT&T produces the Business Circle website, which provides timely and topical blogs, discussions, and solutions for small and midsize businesses. Visitors to the site can learn about everything from business-plan tips and hiring advice to Search Engine Optimization strategies, cybersecurity, and Facebook marketing techniques.

You don't have to be a big brand to excel at content marketing and build an edge for your business. In fact, there are numerous success stories of little known brands that have made a big hit via content development. You may have heard of GoPro, an HD-quality, waterproof, video recording device. The company that manufactures the product made a big splash in 2013 when its customers began uploading video content on YouTube using "GoPro" in the title. The frenzy of activity put GoPro on the map. By 2014, the company had 7.2 million likes on Facebook, 2 million followers on Instagram, and 950,000 Twitter followers. But that's nothing compared to the 1.8 million subscribers it had on YouTube with 450 million views. In essence, GoPro did a masterful job of turning itself into its own media company.

Build the edge for your business with powerful content. Create unique content that people want to share. Tell a story to which people can relate, a narrative they feel like a part of. Then share your content on all the platforms that reach your customers and prospects.

Humanizing the Brand: Storytelling

People love listening to stories. Storytelling needs to be part of your brand's marketing if you are going to humanize your brand and connect with your customers. Storytelling brings your brand to life and makes it more than an institutional entity. And a well-told story helps your customers visualize the experience of your product or service's benefits, often leading to that "aha!" moment.

To craft an effective story you need to know what motivates your customers to buy—and you also need to know what they're buying. Consider the Build-a-Bear Workshop television advertisement. It tells the story of a father and daughter enjoying a holiday moment in one of the stores. It pulls at your heartstrings and makes you want to go there with some special little one in your life. Such stories motivate actions. (More on Build-a-Bear in a moment.)

Another great example of storytelling is the way Steve Jobs introduced the first iPhone. If you haven't seen his presentation, it's worth your time to check it out on YouTube. The story he created had audience members sitting on the edge of their chairs in suspense of what was to come. Jobs kept everyone hanging until he finally revealed the phone that would change the world. Apple continues to tell stories, sharing glimpses of what it looks like for its customers to use their products.

Airbnb also uses stories to build its brand and engage customers. Content on its website features customers' stories demonstrating how real people are experiencing Airbnb service. I personally enjoyed the one about Oscar and Annabelle, a father and daughter. Travel is broadening Annabelle's horizons, plus it's a great way for the two to spend time together sharing experiences. In this hectic, chaotic world, who doesn't want to shut their eyes and dream about an affordable getaway with family or friends?

Missteps Can Be Costly

If you've been in the business world for a while, you've been in meetings where someone eagerly tosses out an idea for a promotion, contest, or marketing campaign to increase sales. It sounds good at the time, and the decision is made to go forward. However, if your brand isn't in tune with your core customers, your good idea could be a huge flop.

For example, in 2010 the Gap rolled out a new logo with the desire to appeal to a trendier crowd. Having been involved in corporate rebranding efforts, I can only imagine how much time and money the company poured into the concept. However, the Gap's core customers were people who wanted the basics and who weren't interested in fashion trends. After only two days, the company returned to the original logo design. As a result of the misstep, many customers lost their connection with the brand because the new logo conveyed a message that the clothing retailer was changing for the worse.

Know What You're Selling: You Aren't in the Widget Business

As you begin to determine your marketing strategies, start by understanding what you're selling. Customers don't come to you because they believe your marketing spin. They come because they want and expect your product or service to satisfy their need. The number of consumers who make decisions based solely on fact is limited. We are all powered by emotions. If you ignore that emotional motivation, you can steer your decision making in the wrong direction. The emotional pull may be one of survival, vanity, love, fear, efficiency, personal growth, etc. You need insight into the customer's motivation to craft the right marketing messages.

Here's a list that touches the main emotional hot buttons you need to push if you're selling a product or service to consumers:

- Happiness or joy
- Health
- Prosperity
- Security
- Relationships with friends and family
- Peace
- Hope for improvement
- Freedom
- Fulfillment
- Confidence
- Longer life
- Sexual companionship
- Comfort

- Approval
- Superiority
- Satisfaction via food

What Is She Really Buying from You?

I've already discussed how Kodak failed in the digital photography world because company leaders buried their heads in the sand and didn't acknowledge the onslaught of this new medium. One aspect that may have contributed to the mindset is that management didn't understand what its customers were actually buying. The film business was lucrative for them, so they were concerned about the bottom-line profits. However, customers weren't buying film and prints; they were buying the ability to preserve memories and tell stories. Think about when you take pictures: weddings, birthdays, family reunions, vacations, and other events. The consumer didn't care whether it was a print photo or a digital one. So the company failed to stay relevant to the customer's needs. As a result, by the time Kodak woke up, it had lost market share, as digital photography steadily became the norm.

You can't sell with slick marketing strategies. What sells a product is the ability to tap into your customers' psyche so they understand that your product or service is precisely what they need.

Look at Build-a-Bear Workshop, whose commercial does a great job mirroring the emotions of its customers. I have collected teddy bears for years, and most of them I've purchased in about the same way. But think about this: I bet you had a special teddy bear at some point in your life that you still remember. It may have been a gift from your parents, a family member, or a close friend.

When Maxine Clark founded Build-a-Bear Workshop, she realized that teddy bears are about memories and experiences. So Build-a-Bear is a place where you take your children, nieces, nephews, and grandchildren to create those special memories. You may have seen the holiday commercial where the little girl looks at her father and says, "You know what the best part of creating my holiday reindeer is?" After a few wrong guesses, she says, "No daddy. The best part is I get to do it with you."

The bear or stuffed animal the child selects looks like any other toy, but looks can be deceiving. Build-a-Bear customers create their own personalized stuffed animals. Instead of going to FAO Schwarz to buy a bear, holiday shoppers line up on Fifth Avenue to get into the Build-a-Bear Workshop. That's the One-Percent Edge.

Think about the hotel business. Hotel operators aren't selling rooms; they are selling a comfortable, safe, and clean place for you to sleep. That's why many of the better hotel chains have invested in top-of-the-line bedding and spa products. One hotel I stayed in offered a menu so I could select the type of pillow(s) I wanted for my stay. Let's just say, I'll be back.

The floral industry struggled during the Great Recession as consumers had less discretionary income. However, one marketing-savvy North Carolina florist fared better than most. Janice Cutler, president of North Raleigh Florist, recognized she wasn't selling flowers; she was selling a sentiment. Cutler's strategy is working. Recently, she opened her second location in Cary, North Carolina.

Get Intimate with Your Customers

Now that you've established your brand promise, identified ways to monitor what your customers want and need, and gotten in tune with what you're selling, it's time to build relationships—to get intimate with your customers. You want people to connect with your brand in a deep and more emotionally satisfying way. The big question is how to get that intimacy without appearing insincere.

Before I go any further, let me tell you what customer intimacy is not. It's not customer service. It isn't a goal to be marked off a list. It has to be earned.

Customer intimacy is about a meaningful engagement. You want to be a partner with your customers. You need to know as much about them as they do about themselves—or more.

For years, brands have talked to customers. It has been a one-way conversation. Companies have pitched their products and had little, if any, interaction with customers. Many have speculated that advertisers placed subliminal messages to manipulate consumers. This myth originated from the 1957 publication of Vance Packard's book *The Hidden Persuaders*. Today, we know these tactics do not work.

The marketing paradigm has shifted significantly. Customers expect two-way, nearly real-time communication. Successful brands are learning how to build these relationships by becoming more humanized, letting customers know that behind the logo there are real people who care about their needs. The relationship with the customer goes well beyond the transaction. Even if your product or service is not something your customer buys frequently—such as a car, television, or house—you need to keep the spark alive.

The first step in creating a campaign to build intimacy is to clearly understand whom you want to talk to and how to reach them. And once again, you need to make sure you completely understand your customer's needs. When you start to see the world as your customer sees it, you have the power to make a recommendation that demonstrates your understanding and your commitment to your customer's success.

Another important element of building intimacy with your customers is to earn their trust. If your market sees your actions as unauthentic, you will have lost the opportunity, perhaps forever. But if you get it right, strong customer intimacy will create a true market advantage. The next time the competition comes knocking at their door, they will want to stick with you.

There are multiple platforms today that you can use to reach your customers. Brands of all sizes can become their own publishing houses. Create content that helps improve the lives of your customers and share it on the multiple channels you have identified. In my opinion, brands that have strong omnichannel customer engagement programs experience better customer retention rates than those who don't.

One of my favorite examples is Chick-fil-A. Over 20 years ago, the company unveiled its billboard campaign that showed a picture of a cow and the slogan "Eat Mor Chikin." The campaign was so popular that the company took the concept to the next level and created an integrated marketing campaign that included television, radio, and social media. But the true *wow* factor here was when the company launched Cow Appreciation Day. The company says more than 900,000 people dressed up. Today, the "cowz" have a dedicated website, they tweet, you can find them on Instagram, they have a Facebook page, and the herd does public appearances.

Chick-fil-A is a brand people have fallen in love with. As a result, its best marketing tools are its customers. They are evangelists for the company. So it should be no surprise that the company earns more revenue per restaurant than any other fast-food chain in the United States, according to *QSR* magazine.[14] Chick-fil-A has the One-Percent Edge.

How can you create that in your business?

Founded in 2010, Made in Mars, Inc., a sports board company, realized the importance of building intimacy with its customers from the beginning. In the "About" section of its Amazon storefront, the company notes its differentiation:

> Looking around we saw a lot of companies in our Biz, many that were doing a good, and sometimes even a great job at making boards and trying to fit into the "Action Sports lifestyle." This was all great, but it just wasn't for us. We want to help our customers who ride and skate our boards define their own lifestyles and make their own paths. We want to be part of your artistic expression, means of transportation and facilitators of good times.[15]

"We always strive to integrate into our customers' experience and be a small part of their life story and adventure," noted Richard Pyles, president and chief creative officer. "Everyone wants to be catered to and have an ongoing and interactive experience. That's what we deliver."[16]

Made in Mars customers stretch across the country, and they are encouraged to give their input for designs and new creations. Made in Mars attributes its success to listening and responding to its customer base, and, as a result, many customers are brand ambassadors in social media. This greatly minimizes the amount of money the company has to spend on advertising and marketing.

"Working with our social media ambassadors is a wonderful way to develop product relatively inexpensively, and it gives us insight into what customers are doing with their boards," Pyles said. "Our ambassadors have essentially co-created this company with their excellent observations and suggestions."[17]

Millennials, who now outnumber baby boomers, expect a two-way conversation with brands.

Immediate gratification and communication are critical to maintaining relevancy for your brand. We live in a world where we barely have to leave our homes for anything. Everything can be ordered online and delivered to our doorstep. And even if we aren't purchasing online, the majority of us research before we make a purchase. That's true for B2B companies as well as B2C. (See more in the sales section in this chapter.)

Today's customers want to build relationships with the brands they buy. They expect a conversation. And in return for improved products and services, 86 percent of millennials are willing to share insights on their consumer habits and decision making processes.[18]

Influencer Marketing

People judge you by the company you keep. That's why another way for brands to create the One-Percent Edge is through influencer marketing. For years, brands have leveraged personalities to pitch their products via television, radio, and print advertising campaigns. But today, the concept of influencer marketing is both more intimate and scalable.

Influencer marketing uses the credibility of or fondness for an individual to reach an audience that relates to that individual. In previous days it was limited to situations such as a well-known athlete speaking for a sports drink. But today, social media has taken this to a new level. Companies can find a YouTube personality to discuss their products. By signing up an influencer, a brand can leverage the credibility and following of a personality that the market knows and trusts. For example, I work with many name brands that want to reach the small business market.

A study by McKinsey found that "marketing-induced consumer-to-consumer word of mouth generates more than twice the sales of paid advertising." And the buyers who were acquired through word-of-mouth had a 37 percent higher retention rate.

Here's one of the most telling numbers: While only 33 percent of consumers trust ads, 90 percent trust peer recommendations. This highlights the nature and importance of social media because in many ways people consider themselves to have some kind of peer relationship with the people they follow via social media.

The first step in influencer marketing is to identify the appropriate influencers for your business in the specific market you want to reach. Some of these key people you may already know, but to broaden your reach you should look for influencers that are not so obvious.

You can use social media tools to find influencers based on keywords or those that belong to specific industry verticals. Additionally, market research techniques can be used to identify influencers using predefined criteria to determine the extent and type of influence. For example, a brand that wants to reach small businesses might follow #smallbiz, #smallbusiness, or #smb. However, if your brand only wants to reach sole proprietors, the focus might narrow to #IC, #freelancer, or #solopreneur.

Keep in mind that it isn't necessarily the quantity of people the influencer touches as it is the quality of engagement. So for example, Justin Bieber has more than 93 million followers on Twitter, but if you have a product for newborns, I doubt many people would be influenced by his endorsement. On the other hand, a mommy blogger may only have 10,000 followers, yet they would be more likely to trust her endorsement and act on it. Instagram influencers with fewer than 1,000 followers reported an 8 percent engagement rate, while those with over 1 million followers engaged with only 1.7 percent of their audience. The research shows 82 percent of people are likely to follow the recommendations of these microinfluencers.[19]

The popularity and significance of influencer marketing will continue to grow as businesses such as yours seek ways to break through the communication clutter and reach customers in more meaningful ways. But collaboration with an influencer and your brand needs to be a win-win. Because the influencer is a trusted source, she will want to ensure you are a legitimate business and your product or service is a good fit for the audience. When a company approaches me, I spend a considerable amount of time vetting it. My platform is too important for me to risk alienating my followers by pushing something at them that doesn't make sense or that I wouldn't use myself.

The same is true for your business. Before you engage with an influencer, do your due diligence. Is this someone you truly want your brand to be associated with? Does the individual have integrity, or is she just a pitch artist? How established is she in her market? Is her following real? Check sites such as Klout.com that measure the reach of the influencer in social media markets and TwitterAudit.com to see if followers are real people.

Many influencers expect compensation for their recommendation of your product or service, however, the Federal Trade Commission has cracked down on this. If there is valuable consideration exchanged for the mention of your product, the influencer must disclose that information. Some influencers may recommend your product or service because they truly believe in it. This is known as an earned influencer recommendation. For example, I set up a video studio in my home and I spent time on YouTube listening to experts explain which products were best and how to use them. They were sharing their expertise in terms of what works well for them, which helped me determine the right equipment for my needs.

The Critical Keys to Judging Your Social Media Marketing Effectiveness

As recently as 2014, business writers were talking about social media marketing as the next big thing. Today, it's hard to imagine any business that doesn't invest a lot of time, and sometimes money, in social media marketing.

However, despite our wide acceptance and reliance on it, in order to build and maintain the One-Percent Edge, it's important to occasionally take a step back and try to get a handle on our social media marketing effectiveness. This can help you discover which strategies are working the best, uncover those that are letting you down, and refocus your efforts for increased cost effectiveness and growth.

The bottom line is that you need to make assessments based on your return on investment. This gets a little tricky because you may not have a number immediately assigned to every element that goes into your social media marketing efforts. This is especially true for smaller businesses where a DIY social media marketing approach is in place. For example, how do you value your time?

Value Time Invested

If you personally handle elements of or all of your social media marketing program, there are two ways to put a number on your time. First, you can estimate how much it would cost you to hire someone to do what you currently do. That's pretty easy and straightforward. A second approach would be to consider the lost opportunities you're experiencing due to the hours you spend on social media marketing and assign a number to that.

Merely taking the time to make these two estimates will tell you something about the current state of your social media marketing effectiveness. If the value of your lost opportunities is greater than what you would pay someone to do your social media marketing work, you need to farm it out as soon as possible.

One more area to consider when you're calculating your costs: paid social media marketing and the various subscription services you may be using. In a spreadsheet, you would have two columns, one for organic social media marketing and one for paid social media marketing, or you might call these social media ads. Judging your return on investment on the paid ads won't be difficult, but be sure to include the time and money you or your team spend planning them.

Once you're happy with the figures, you'll need to consider your goals and your progress against your goals. Are you building a following? If so, then you can quickly determine the cost of each new follower? Are you looking for a boost in sales? In that case, you need to be able to track sales back to followers. Do you want to build your influence? You need to assign a value on opportunities that have opened up to you because of your social media clout.

Maintain Consistency

I'll be the first to admit that some of these numbers will be fuzzy. That's okay if you keep two things in mind:

- You need to be consistent in the values you assign. Once you set them, stick with them.

- You're looking for trends and cause and effect in the numbers over time.

Next, I'll explain these two points and why they are important for gauging your social media marketing effectiveness.

Let me use the government's monthly unemployment figures as an example. It doesn't matter if April's unemployment rate was exactly 5.6 percent. What's important is that it was collected and measured using the same means and criteria as were used in January, February, and March. When there is consistency, the numbers will reflect trends along with cause and effect. We can make rational decisions.

When you take a social media effectiveness snapshot like this at regular intervals, you'll be creating a valuable database of relevant statistics.

Social media has become such an integral part of our everyday lives and business habits that many business owners, small and big, fail to measure their social media marketing effectiveness, especially when they are doing everything themselves or have piled the duties onto other team members. Unless they are paying to boost posts, they figure their expenses are too small to bother with.

That may be true in one sense, but unless you measure the effectiveness of social media marketing, you will never be able to discover the strategies that work well for you and those that don't. This, of course, will seriously hamper your ability to grow your business.

Marketing and Sales

Your marketing and sales teams should work together. For some reason, in almost every company, there is a disconnect between the two. The marketing team is busy spreading the word about the brand, and the sales team may or may not even know what the messaging is.

Marketing should arm sales with what it's hearing via various marketing platforms and what its research is telling it in terms of customer needs and motivations. Sales, on the other hand, should inform the marketing team with the feedback it gets from customers. Both groups will benefit from the exchange, as will the overall results for your company.

When there is a disconnect between the two departments, your company loses opportunities and wastes money, which can impact your brand image. Along with a colleague, I put together a yearlong, major campaign for a well-known brand to reach the small and midsize business market. Although the company didn't know its cost of customer acquisition, its conversion rates, or the lifetime value of a customer, we were able to extrapolate conservative numbers and demonstrate that the company would have a significant return on investment. The marketing team was all over the concept, but the executive team declined. Why? Not because the executives didn't see the value in the program, but because they had no process to ensure the sales leads generated from the program would be followed up on and closed. They had no means of tracking because the sales and marketing teams did not collaborate.

A company with the One-Percent Edge has teams that collaborate and recognize their common goal. They meet regularly and they have access to integrated technology that easily gets leads into the right hands and provides a means for reporting results. This information helps marketing adjust its messages and strategies.

Sales with the One-Percent Edge

Whether you're a B2B or B2C organization, your customers and prospects know a lot about your products and services before they ever connect with you. Because they have done their homework, you should too. Life happens at warp speed today, and time is a limited resource. Don't waste your customers' time. Do sufficient research so you have a clear understanding of their needs.

That's particularly true for B2B companies. There was a time when you could cold call a prospect, get an appointment, and meet to introduce your product or service. Those days are gone. In order to earn that appointment, to get in front of a prospect, you've got a lot of work to do.

First, you need to know as much as you can about the prospect's business. Does it use products like yours? If so, with whom is it currently doing business? Can you provide something more valuable? What problems and challenges does the company appear to have? How can you enhance its business and be a true partner in its success?

When I was the CEO and cofounder for my Internet company, a young woman from a local bank approached me and asked if her regional manager and she could meet with me to discuss how the bank could serve my business. Reluctantly, I agreed. (Remember, everyone is crazy busy.) When we met, she dived into her pitch about all the bank's capabilities without asking me about our current banking relationships and needs. However, the pièce de résistance was when she pulled out a flyer and began to tell me about all the organizations for women business owners in the area. I listened politely, but on the inside I was laughing. Not only was I aware of the organizations, but I was on the national boards of many of them as well. She didn't get my business, and quite honestly she wasted my time.

The days of the boilerplate sales presentation are history. Sales guru Brian Tracy says that ultimately all selling is relationship selling, and that underscores the importance of the sales dialogue. Relationships develop when you get to know someone.

The hosts of late night talk shows may use monologues to get the evening off to a good start, but in sales, it's the dialogue that will serve as the foundation of a successful relationship between a buyer and a seller.

Because there is so much information on the Internet about your business and your product, your customers may be almost ready to make buying decisions before you get in front of them. They have read the online reviews and checked out your competition. So it's up to you not to screw it up.

Here are the facts:

- Your customer's problem is more important than what you're selling.
- Your customer must be assured that you understand the problem.
- You must build trust with your customer in order to have your sales pitch met with receptive ears.
- You should be able to simply and concisely explain why you have the best solution to your customer's problem.

As easy as this sounds, it can be difficult to do. After all, sales professionals should believe that they have an excellent product or service and they are eager to share that with people because they know it will make their customers' lives better. However, you can't "sell" anything. Your customers buy what they want and need.

Have you ever met someone for the first time and walked away from your encounter thinking, "Wow, that person seemed to really care about me"? If you have, I'll guarantee you it was because the person asked questions about you and listened to your answers. If you do that, it puts you in the position to ask follow-up questions, which prove that you're listening to the person who is doing the talking. Follow-up questions are great for closing the loop of understanding.

I have a friend who used to be a newspaper reporter. He was trained to ask questions, listen to answers, and ask follow-up questions. This is how he handles most social encounters, but he always notices when the people he's talking to don't ask him a question. He's explained to me that he expects this because people are their own favorite subjects to talk about. However, he takes special note when someone shows interest (or curiosity) by asking him questions.

With his newspaper training, he's somewhat more consciously aware of the interest people take in him during conversations. However, we all process this information and store it, even if it is done unconsciously.

When you're meeting new prospects, you have only one chance to make a first impression that shows you're interested in their concerns and not there to wow them with a sales demonstration or slick spiel. It's your responsibility to start and lead a sales dialogue.

Ask Questions

In your own words, repeat what was just said and be sure you understand properly, and then ask follow-up questions.

Work your solution to your prospect's problem naturally into the sales dialogue. If you begin to build the foundation of the relationship first, the relationship will be much stronger in the long run and result in more sales.

Listening instead of selling also allows you to position your sales pitch based on the issues and concerns that matter most to your customer. If you've ever attended a timeshare sales presentation then you've witnessed this firsthand. They start off by getting you to "like" them while you enjoy a lavish buffet breakfast. Then they tour you around the property, getting more and more information about you the entire time. They are masterful at asking questions so you talk about your travel interests, the amount of time you have to travel, and who you normally travel with. Then they pivot their presentation to entice you with just the right offering. They are relentless in their efforts to keep repositioning the package to get you to say yes. And after you've seen them run the numbers in numerous ways, they explain that the pricing is only available now. If you walk away, then you don't get the deal. The original ninety-minute presentation can turn into a half a day or more. Whew.

The problem with timeshare salespeople, however, is that while they are agile in their sales approach, they really don't care whether it's a good deal for the customer. For them, the sale is a goal, not an outcome.

A company with the One-Percent Edge combines relationship building, listening, and agility, but the sale is a natural outcome of being the right solution for the client. If, after listening to the customer and her needs, you don't think you have the right solution, be honest. Don't try to sell something that isn't a good fit.

While I was writing today, a man came to clean the carpet in one of my upstairs bedrooms and my master bedroom. When he arrived, I showed him the master bedroom and he said, "You don't want to clean this carpeting." I was shocked. He explained that it is a high-grade carpet and cleaning it too frequently could cause the seams to begin to separate.

I couldn't believe how honest he was. I wanted the carpet cleaned, and I think a lot of companies would have done the job, taken my money, and not said a word. I thanked him for his honesty, and I will definitely recommend him to others in my neighborhood.

Internal Marketing

The importance of external marketing is obvious, but most companies miss the importance of internal marketing. It's as important for your team to love your brand as it is for your customers. Without that connection, employees can actually undermine your marketing messages. Individuals who don't understand your value and believe in your brand can do serious damage to customer relations. But when employees embrace your brand, they are more loyal and invested in the success of your business.

You probably have some sort of employee communication already in place to share company news, but if it is like most I'm familiar with, it doesn't "market" your business to your team. By employing principles used in external marketing, you can share with your team what makes your brand special. Create positive energy around new products, programs, and initiatives by helping them see the big vision. Employees should hear the same messaging as your customers.

When I led a marketing department, I was involved in numerous internal campaigns. We distributed thousands of posters with the company's mission statement and core values. Employees were given laminated cards reinforcing the core values. We produced videos and banners, but the most effective strategy was the personal touch. We found that a roundtable discussion with a high-level executive who could personally explain the vision did a lot to energize and engage employees.

Once you have your goals, they must be communicated. However, sending out a memo one day and then moving on won't accomplish that. Simplify your messaging. Make it a mantra. Model it and mention it. Your employees should be able to recite your goals back to you. Quiz them on it: "What's the most important thing we're trying to accomplish this quarter?" If they can't answer that question, it's not their fault—it's your fault.

Internal marketing is particularly important when you're experiencing change in your organization. In other words, as you implement the One-Percent Edge process, internal marketing assists in keeping everyone aligned and in sync with the goals. Otherwise, change can be unsettling, and employees often become disengaged and disgruntled.

CHAPTER 7

The Process Edge

"Every problem in business is the result of a systems
  dysfunction."

—BRIAN RAZZAQUE

So far I have written about leadership, products, people, marketing, and customer service. Each of these is integral for the success and sustainability of your business. However, you can't work on these elements without also striving for excellence and adaptability in your business operations. Each aspect of your business is interdependent on the other; a failure to be agile and innovative in one area will derail your overall success.

Technology is a big part of your business process, but process is bigger than your IT. Think of it like the internal workings of a clock or an engine: Do the parts work smoothly together to deliver the end result? Companies that best use technology to meet the ever-changing needs of consumers as well as business operations will be the winners.

- Are our internal processes streamlined?
- Are we wasting time and money on redundant activities?
- What eats up most of the time for our team? Is there a way to introduce technology?
- In an ideal world, what would we need to increase our productivity?
- What could be done to enhance our service levels?
- What could be done to improve business development?
- Are we collecting big data in a way to improve operations and product delivery?
- Are we giving our customers a voice?
- Are we collecting the data to help make strategic decisions?

- Are our internal processes in sync?
- Do our marketing and sales organizations mesh?
- Do our processes reflect our brand appropriately and deliver consistently?
- How can our internal processes enhance the overall customer experience?

Achieving the One-Percent Edge is impossible with outdated modes of operations and technologies. Think of it as like being in quicksand: No matter how hard you try to move, it slowly sucks you down. In fact, the harder and faster you try to work your way out of it, the worse your situation gets. Business leaders who have made significant investments in old systems or equipment may be reluctant to pursue fresher, more relevant investments. There are many reasons for this, ranging from price of authorship to ego. However, even with the best ideas and a strong commitment to new business opportunities, your internal infrastructure must be able to support your growth.

We have all seen the illustrations that show the evolution of man. They start with a short, hunched-over, apelike creature with long arms and get progressively more erect and taller until they look like us. The same kind of progress should be reflected in the evolution of the processes or systems upon which your business is built.

By default, your processes will start out on a rather crude footing, and this isn't a bad thing. The strategy of "fake it until you make it" can serve start-ups and service-providing companies experimenting with a new venture quite well. In fact, this approach serves well to illustrate how your business systems should be constantly evolving. Here's an example:

Let's say you think you have a better approach to testing job applicants to see if their personalities are a good match for various company cultures, but you aren't sure how big the demand is or exactly how your potential clients will respond to your service. You envision a cloud-based system where companies answer some

THE PROCESS EDGE / 169

questions about the culture and then software analyzes the input to create a series of questions that will be given to job applicants. The software would then score all the applicants based on how well their answers harmonized with the company culture.

While you know how to rate applicant responses, and you understand the psychological metrics and the thinking that drives the questions, it will take a sizable investment to translate all of that to a cloud-based artificial intelligence software system. But you don't want to risk your funds or find a funding source this early in the project.

Instead, you decide to launch a website with your first system built in: a web-based interface that quizzes founders and others about their company culture. While you market the site and work with your first few clients, you'll do the rest of the steps manually, either on your own or by farming the tasks out to others who are competent in this area.

If it looks like demand is high enough and that you'll be able to charge the rate structure you envision, you'll begin building the rest of the automated systems, and before long you'll have the entire project systematized.

In this case, those first clients don't know how you're handling the back end of your service, and they don't need to know. In fact, you want them to be under the impression that you have your system developed. Your clients don't need to know how hard and fast you're working behind the scenes. And it's the same for developing systems in any business for any business process.

Your systems need to be constantly evolving. If you put a system in place and then think, "Phew! I'm glad that's done," you're thinking wrong. That's an easy trap to fall into. Developing a system can take a lot of effort, and it's not appealing to think that you may need to go back and redo it in the near future.

Failing to constantly evolve your systems and processes can deliver a death blow to your company. Most of us know the history of U.S. automakers that for decades were content with selling the most cars and making few process improvements. In the 1970s,

Japanese automakers—using quality control systems developed by American engineers—began making cars that were superior in quality to U.S. models. In fact, within one generation of consumers, Japanese manufacturers turned the phrase "Made in Japan" from a disparaging remark to a mark of excellence.

It has been nearly fifty years since Japanese automakers began to outshine U.S. automakers in quality and reliability. In recent decades, American cars have improved greatly, even winning top honors in many categories. However, overcoming the reputation for slipshod manufacturing processes has been difficult. Consumer sentiment doesn't turn on a dime.

This is why your commitment to continual process evolution must be unwavering.

Yet, there are human factors that weigh against change. The U.S. automakers, for example, were so satisfied with today's success that they didn't invest in tomorrow's success. Further, as I recently pointed out, you—or whoever originally designed the system or process—have a certain amount of ego invested in it, so it's natural to be reluctant when others suggest changes. This brings us to our next important point on developing processes and systems: Everyone needs to participate.

It's critical to create a culture that brings everyone on board, enabled, and empowered to create and improve systems. This is true because:

▶ **Conditions change.** Markets are always evolving. U.S. auto buyers were satisfied with Detroit quality levels until they experienced higher levels of quality and reliability with Japanese cars.

▶ **People change.** When Jane was in charge of accounting, she made some great process changes. But now that Jane has been bumped upstairs and John has been brought on, he has a different perspective and sees some opportunities for improvement that Jane missed.

▶ **Desired end results change.** You will find ways to modify your product or service. It may be to improve it, or make it more desirable for a new market segment. If we view process improvement driven by your employees as bottom-up improvement, there will also be some top-down improvements. Don't try to cobble together tomorrow's product with today's process.

Processes and Human Factors

Few people like to be stuck in a rigid system. This is often the criticism people hurl at companies that are overly systematized. Employees complain about being turned into robots or not being able to express themselves. This problem can be overcome if members of your team understand that no process is cast in stone, everything is open for improvement, and, in fact, their participation in making those improvements is encouraged.

We talk about the need for instilling an entrepreneurial spirit in larger or established organizations. This happens naturally when you create a culture that has everyone asking the question, "How can we do this better?"

After all, isn't that the single most important question for an entrepreneur? The foundational attitude of a successful entrepreneur is to examine a product or service and find a better way to provide it, or to look at a situation and explore how to solve a problem. Transfer that attitude into micromoments within your organization and you're well on your way to creating the most efficient and responsive company in your industry.

And the benefits stretch even further. In Chapter 5, about leveraging "The People Edge," we discussed the value of creating brand ambassadors. You'll never have brand ambassadors if you don't have employees buying into what your company is doing. One of the benefits of having everyone working together to evolve systems is that when an individual's improvement suggestion is incorporated, that person immediately takes some ownership of the organization. And it is human nature to exhibit pride of ownership—a necessary part of brand ambassadorship.

Process for Consistency

Perhaps it sounds counterintuitive to talk about process in a book about being agile and innovative. However, attaining the One-Percent Edge is a process in and of itself. Highly successful companies build processes so they can consistently deliver their product or service to their customers. It's only through a structured thought process that you can measure tangible results.

For smaller organizations, I always coach leaders to think about a process that is teachable, repeatable, and consistently delivered. Your customers want to trust that they will get the same quality of service each time they do business with you. For example, I used to love eating at a particular deli in New York City. A few years ago, I went in to grab some chopped liver. While everything looked the same, the food wasn't even close to what I'd experienced before. That's when I learned the restaurant had changed ownership. I tried it one more time and was disappointed again, so I never went back.

Process for Quality

"Do what you do so well that they will want to see it again and bring their friends."

—WALT DISNEY

You may have heard the old saying that you are only as good as what you did for me yesterday. Your business may have an amazing track record of success with a customer, but it's the one misstep that can ruin the relationship going forward. If you fail to consistently deliver on your quality and service promises, your customers will go somewhere else. Today's consumers are increasingly reluctant to give businesses second chances.

What checks and balances do you have to ensure every interaction is delivered with the same exceptional quality? Think about all the restaurants in the heart of New York City. You can find any type of food your heart desires. Yet many tourists who visit the city won't take a risk on an unknown establishment. That's why you'll see well-known chains such as McDonald's, Applebee's, Pizza Hut, Starbucks, and Dunkin' Donuts bustling. Diners know exactly what to expect because the food is the same no matter if you're in New York City or Louisville, Kentucky. Product consistency is the key.

Let me shine a light on one more aspect of this. Consumers have developed a relationship with these global chains. The primary goal of your organization is to create long-term relationships. How valuable are these relationships? I've seen one estimate that pegs the lifetime value of a Starbucks customer at more than $14,000. I'm certain that all of these big brands also have astronomically high LTVs. My point is that consistency is a major building block in the relationships these companies enjoy with consumers. The return on investment on consistency is impressive.

The only way you can guarantee your products and service delivery will be the same each time is by ensuring that all of your employees maintain the same standards, abide by the same policies and procedures, and use the same processes, practices, and systems to perform their jobs at the desired level.

Process isn't only necessary for your product/service delivery. You need processes to train your team, to manage your accounting, to work with vendors, to manage vacation schedules, to conduct sales, and to manage your marketing. In small firms, process helps you stay on track. For larger organizations, process should make dealing with divergent departments and even cultures seamless. You may have done business with an organization where one group or division manages a process one way while another one has its own operational procedures.

Don't Reinvent the Wheel

When everyone in your organization understands how a process works in your company, there will be no need to reinvent the wheel. But a hodgepodge of methodologies will lead to redundancy. That's when critical items can fall through the cracks. A friend who worked in IT for a large financial services firm learned that many of his vendor contracts had not been countersigned. When he discussed the situation with his legal department, they were under the impression it was his department's job to get that, while his team thought that legal was taking care of it. There was no process to ensure the work was completed.

Time Tracking

Knowing how your team is spending time is an important insight to gain. So it's time for good old time tracking. This is important so you can understand how productive your business is and if you need to make adjustments.

Don't forget to account for Parkinson's Law: "Work expands so as to fill the time available for its completion." One woman I worked with in the corporate world came up to my office nearly every morning with her coffee, sat down, and struck up a conversation. Her little visits took a chunk out of my day. So you need to get a handle on how much time various aspects of your internal processes are taking and evaluate whether it's appropriate for the task.

I've done time tracking in a corporate setting and in my own businesses. It's a revealing exercise. Is your team spending time on the right things? Depending on the size and type of your business, you may be able to do this with a software program. However, it can also be done via an honor system. Ask employees to keep track of the time much the same way as attorneys and consultants do. This will arm you with the information you need to adjust your operations accordingly and increase productivity. You might be surprised how much time is wasted on noncritical business functions. For example, are employees spending too much time on emails? Perhaps there is a team member who struggles with some aspects of his job. Shifting responsibilities could improve outcomes.

Time tracking also gives you a glimpse at how often your team is interrupted and distracted from the task at hand. Short interruptions aren't bad and generally don't affect productivity. However, when employees shift from one project to another it takes a considerable amount of time to change their thinking and get focused on something new. Workers may believe that multitasking means they are getting more done, but organizational experts disagree. If you're a multitasker, you may have noticed that when you jump from one project to another, by the time you get back to the original project, you've forgotten where you were.

When you enhance your infrastructure processes you'll be better equipped to direct the time and talents of your team to focus on growth and innovation. Some companies ask employees to schedule quiet time. During this period of the day, they disconnect from emails, phones, and other external distractions to concentrate on a particular aspect of their job responsibilities. This concept is more conducive for knowledge workers but can also be helpful for most any position.

"You can make a lot of mistakes and still recover if you run an efficient operation. Or you can be brilliant and still go out of business if you're too inefficient."

—SAM WALTON, Walmart founder

The Automated Agile Company

Basically, anything in your company that can be automated should be. Time is money. Whenever you can automate a process internally, if frees you up for business development. Think about all the tasks that used to be completed manually that are now managed with technology solutions.

I recently purchased a new phone at an AT&T store. The sales associate asked me what color I'd like, and when I told him, he quickly looked up the inventory availability on his iPad to make sure it was in stock. (You don't run a business where employees have to tell customers, "Let me check in the back to see if we have that," do you?) Technology is empowering employees with information at their fingertips that improves their productivity and gives them the opportunity to focus on the customer. In fact, technology has streamlined the entire sales process. Not only does it help salespeople become more productive, but it also enhances the entire customer experience.

Using the One-Percent Edge process, review what your company is doing internally. Are there ways to introduce more technology to improve overall business operations? While this book does not discuss all the programs that are available to your business, it is important that you're constantly evaluating and upgrading to stay ahead of the curve in your industry. What changes are occurring that could affect your business? As I mentioned at the beginning of the chapter, outdated technology and processes will slow your business growth. If you're shopping for a state-of-the-art telephone system, would you want to do business with a company that still uses an old-fashioned answering machine?

As part of a study commissioned by AT&T, researchers at the Cambridge Judge Business School in the United Kingdom interviewed senior executives from a variety of sectors across the globe to find the common strategies that helped their companies innovate successfully to meet burgeoning trends in technology. What they discovered was that innovation occurs when business models match up with one or more of the six patterns where technological advances overlap with market needs, thus resulting in growth and transformation. The six patterns of overlap between technology and market needs are:

▶ **Tailor-made products and services:** Meeting customers' individual needs, such as online retailers' recommendation services

▶ **Sustainability:** Minimizing waste and managing resource costs, such as companies that harvest and recycle parts

▶ **Jointly owned assets:** Boosting efficiency and lowering costs, such as in peer-to-peer businesses

▶ **Paying only for a service that is used:** Saving money when possible; for example, by using car-share companies

▶ **Effective monitoring of supply chains:** Using handheld tracking systems to better monitor the supply chain, such as support-service companies

▶ **Using data to easily adapt to customer needs:** Staying fast on your feet; for example, clothing companies that maintain less inventory so they can quickly produce new designs to meet fashion trends

"You can see technology and innovation changing every industry," said Steve McGaw, AT&T chief marketing officer. "We're always trying to better understand the mechanics of innovation, so we can help companies lead their industries."[1]

Moving with Mobile

Mobility is exploding and transforming every business paradigm. In every industry and sector, mobile technologies are displacing older means of doing work and reaching out to customers. Enterprises that leverage mobility will experience significant operational benefits, such as enhanced productivity, reduced costs, and better customer experience. However, as a business leader you must be prepared to make the necessary and appropriate organizational changes. Old methods must be switched to digitally powered ones, and your challenge is the fact that the landscape is always changing.

Consider some of the many ways technology is transforming the way we do business today, and consider how your company can benefit from them.

Nordstrom's "Text to Buy" Program: This is an industry first. It leverages the relationship between Nordstrom customers and the Nordstrom employee who is their salesperson or personal stylist. The Nordstrom employee uses a custom text message app to share curated fashion suggestions with the customer, who can then make a purchase via a simple text message response.

Restaurants Using iPad Ordering for Customers: A win-win for the customer and the restaurant. The technology reduces the amount of staff the restaurant needs and increases throughput. Further, diners appreciate the opportunity to order more quickly, get their meal, and pay their bill. The technology helps restaurants significantly reduce costs. In 2016, restaurants that adopted mobile ordering pads saw their revenue increase upward of 360 percent, according to CAKE, an integrated restaurant technology platform. One restaurant manager said that before using the point-of-sale system, his team guessed that the staff gave out approximately $400 a month in comps. After switching to the program, which captured the real figure, they were shocked to learn it was more like $4,000 a month. It also enhances the customer experience by reducing the number of errors in food orders, which also drive up costs.

Self-Serve Airline Kiosks Reduce Operational Costs: The cost of a DIY transaction is pennies compared to a live service interaction. Furthermore, travelers appreciate the opportunity to skip the long lines at ticket counters. Similarly, grocery store chains and other retailers are moving to self-checkout technologies, freeing the traditional cashiers to manage other tasks such as restocking the shelves or helping customers.

The Amazon Dash Replenishment Service: Just say it, scan it, or press a specially provided button, and Dash reorders a consumable item that you regularly have to reorder. Pushing technology even further, recently Amazon revealed the long-awaited details about its new physical grocery store concept called Amazon Go. The new store is touted to eliminate checkout lines and allow customers to enter the store using a mobile app and then simply take items off shelves, put them in their carts, and roll out the front door when finished shopping. Is this the next generation of grocery stores?

While I've focused on retail, you should consider how these technologies could be applied to your business. Service companies can benefit from technology by limiting back-office time and giving employees in the field access to critical information at their fingertips. For example, my HVAC service company equips every representative with a mobile device so he can review with the customer the last time a unit was serviced and when filters need to be changed.

Balancing High Tech and High Touch

Technology provides efficiency and lowers costs, but it must be balanced against the customer service aspect of your business operations. How often are your customers frustrated because they can't reach a real person or identify the appropriate method of lodging a complaint or obtaining assistance?

Technology can enhance the high-touch aspect of your business. Take the Four Seasons Hotel, for example, a chain known for its upscale service. It has a mobile app, which at first blush seems odd, but the app complements the human-touch aspect of the firm's brand. It's available for customers to use when they want to, or they can choose not to. It also offers some features that make it easier for guests to manage their stay including a GPS for the area and a way to request housekeeping services.

Your challenge as a business leader is to incorporate technology to enhance your operations, but you must be very careful not to interfere with the customer experience. Saving money with efficiencies may mean losing revenue by driving customers away.

Should Others Provide Your IT Processes?

There is a new layer of processes in virtually every business today: online processes. In other words, companies are achieving competitive advantage through access to assets rather than investing capital to own them. This is a significant shift for businesses of all sizes, but particularly for small companies.

Software as a Service (SaaS) is booming. These cloud-based services are filling the needs of a great many companies, big and small. Examples of popular cloud services include:

- Social media management
- Customer relationship management
- Collaboration

Additionally, there are online processes available that do the job of many legacy local computer-based (or even people-based) processes, such as accounting and finance, inventory control, scheduling, project management, and customer service.

Firms today face the question of whether to build their own custom solutions to provide these services or replace their legacy systems with an established SaaS provider. The financial benefit is that your business can buy as much of the service as it needs.

Customer relationship management is a good example. Your cost depends on how many users you have. If you're a start-up and have a sales and marketing team of three people, you'll just pay for a few users. However, when you start to grow, you can up your contract to include more users. In the same way, if your business model changes or you implement efficiencies that allow you to reduce the number of users you need, you can dial back your contract.

Homegrown software solutions usually aren't this flexible. If you need to get a developer on board to increase the capacity of your system, the price can run quite high. Additional changes down the line lead to more developer fees and an increasingly complex custom solution. Many businesses find that they are essentially painting themselves into a corner when they create their own software solutions, so approach any DIY IT project cautiously.

Process Improvements Deliver Intangible Benefits

However, more often than not, improving the efficiency of your processes will be beneficial, even when unexpected.

We have already touched on the importance of establishing and maintaining relationships with your customers. The processes your company employs can affect these relationships. Back in the day when the big three Detroit automakers reigned supreme, families would often identify as a "Chevy family" or "Ford family"; they would only drive those brands. Ultimately, that's the kind of relationship and loyalty you want to establish with your customers or clients.

These strong relationships, the reputation of your business, and the goodwill associated with it are intangible. They can be difficult or impossible to measure. And when we talk about processes, it's easy to frame the conversation simply in the tangible terms of efficiency, cost savings, return on investment, and bottom-line improvements.

However, many times when we set out to pursue a tangible, measurable process improvement, it creates an intangible—yet extremely valuable—benefit. You need to consider this as you're planning improvements. When you focus only on the immediately measureable results of a process improvement, you aren't seeing the big picture.

If, for example, you have the money to make one process improvement but there are two things you'd like to accomplish, after you complete the spreadsheet analysis, decide which will have the greater impact on building stronger customer relationships. If there is no concrete way to attach a number to this, go with your gut instincts; listen to what your experience is telling you.

Consumers know Amazon by its Internet presence. The design of its website, by the way, never wins any awards. However, it's not the colors, layout, and graphics that we see on the screens of our devices that's most important to Amazon's success. It may be the hard work and innovations it has achieved in the infrastructure and logistics of warehousing and fulfillment that are its greatest assets, at least on the e-commerce side of its business.

The speed and accuracy with which it takes orders, packages them, and ships them out is astounding. Amazon has automated a lot of processes in its fulfillment operation and is deploying robots to handle as much of the work as possible.

The consumer does not see any of this, but Amazon has orchestrated all the moving parts of its warehousing and shipping operation so well that its customers can order without any worries. If you were around in the earlier days of e-commerce, you know that engendering trust in the process was a major hurdle that had to be cleared. By constantly improving and innovating processes, Amazon has created millions of brand-loyal online shoppers; the company's tangible investment has paid off big time in intangible results with shoppers.

Further, taking initiatives that demonstrate your leadership, commitment to innovation, and position as a company that is going places will foster interest in and ultimately loyalty to your company. It's human nature to want to be associated with recognized leaders. It starts in elementary school when everyone wants to hang out with the cool kids, and it continues through adulthood. We see it in our political leadership; even people with a lot of money and influence want to rub elbows with those who have a little more money and influence.

If you take the tangible steps of investing in process improvements that will make your company a recognized leader in your industry, you'll find that it becomes easier for you to work with vendors and perhaps even acquire more customers. For example, if vendors sense that you are on track to be the biggest, most important player in the game, they will want to establish good relationships with you today. This can empower you to get better terms than you would otherwise receive. Your tangible investment in improvements will pay dividends in increased goodwill.

Before we leave the topic on how process can enhance your customer's experience, I need to make the point that there is another side to this coin. Making the tangible mistake of not investing in process improvements and innovations can have the intangible result of ruining loyalty and goodwill.

I began this discussion by mentioning the old phenomenon of "Chevy families" and "Ford families." Detroit's failure to adequately invest in processes that would produce tangible improvements in automobile quality killed a lot of that brand loyalty. Previously, many car buyers had an ingrained and subconscious attitude that they would buy only American cars. Failing to improve processes shattered that attitude.

Practical Suggestions

The simple checklist is an unsung hero among processes and systems. It can be born from a documented process to make sure all the steps are followed, or creating a checklist can be the first step in developing/documenting a process. Let's look at this second point.

We talk about turn-key businesses. The term is often used to describe and market a franchise. The implication is that the franchisor has developed all the processes and systems required to support the business. I suggest that in most cases, the first step in the development of these processes and systems is the creation of checklists.

A checklist will standardize a legacy procedure. Let's say you commit to standardizing and improving the processes that run your business. (By the way, don't limit this merely to customer-facing processes; include all the internal systems that contribute to overhead costs.) It's a good idea to start by having your team members create checklists for what they do. This simple step pays off in no fewer than four ways by:

- Forcing employees to think about what they do
- Giving you documents you can use to train others
- Providing you with a picture of what people are actually doing, rather than what you think they are doing, which gives you a tool to make efficiencies
- Serving as a blueprint for automation to follow

After a checklist is created, a good next step is to flesh out the process even further by creating a more formal procedure that defines the process. If you want to use a time-proven and almost universally understood system accomplishing this, base your system on the simple recipe card.

We have all followed cooking recipes, so we're familiar with the general format, and we certainly understand their purpose. For any given process, you need to list the required materials, give the steps in order, and collect any special tips and observations that will help the person who is trying to "follow the recipe." And if you've ever looked at recipe cards that have been handed down through generations of a family, you're certain to find various notes that have been jotted down, so allow for comments and corrections by other than the original author.

Where you are in the evolution of your company, as well as the kind of procedure that you're dealing with, will direct you toward the system required to control the "recipes" that capture your processes. Formal document-control procedures will be necessary for some high-level processes, but much of what we're discussing here are the nuts and bolts of getting the simpler, everyday tasks done in the most efficient and repeatable manner possible. In those cases, a less bureaucratic solution is preferred.

I suggest you explore creating a local wiki to capture these. There are plenty of free wiki software packages available that are easy and fun to use. Creating your own "Daily Process Wiki" would keep everything in one place, allow you to standardize how processes are explained, capture edits by all your team members, and make it easy for you to scroll through and review what hoops employees are jumping through in order to get things done. Once your team has done a good job capturing their tasks in the wiki, it can also be used as a tool for cross-training.

Before we I close this section on process, let me share one more point that underscores the importance of documenting your processes: If you plan to sell your business someday or turn it into a franchise, having an excellent collection of documented processes and procedures will enhance the value of your business and make it much easier to either sell or prepare for franchising.

CHAPTER 8

The Financial Edge

"If you can't measure it, you can't control it."

—**MEG WHITMAN**

A s the country was technically pulling out of what we now call the Great Recession, I read a report that said nearly half of all business owners and business leaders believed that the economy was preventing them from growing their businesses. Really? I can't remember a time when there weren't complaints about the economy. Companies with the One-Percent Edge understand how to make money and remain relevant in any economy. How? They listen to the story their numbers are telling them.

- Are we drilling down into our financials to truly understand what is happening within our organization?
- Are profit margins slipping? If so, are there ways to correct the trend before it's too late?
- Do we have excess capacity we could turn into revenue opportunities?
- Are we pricing appropriately, or are we leaving money on the table? In other words, are we constantly competing on price alone?
- Could outsourcing improve our overall financial picture and provide great agility in our operations?
- Do we know who our most profitable customers are, and are we focused on them?
- Are we making the mistake of relying on historical financial data to make real-time decisions?
- Do we have an accurate picture of the cost of customer acquisition and the lifetime value of our customers?

⯈ Are we making the right investments in talent?

⯈ Are we focusing too much on top-line growth (growth for growth's sake) while jeopardizing the health of our bottom line?

Unfortunately, too many business leaders in companies of all sizes are myopic in their focus on revenues and profits alone. The alarming fact is that your company may be in the black, but there could be huge missed opportunities or profitability leaks because you aren't drilling down to understand what's driving the revenue and what may be bogging it down. You may be surprised to learn that your best client or customer or your most popular product may actually be costing you money. Recall that you may need to fire customers who are:

- Taking up too much time
- Being disruptive
- Constantly in arrears
- Always demanding special treatment

Firing a customer is obviously not a choice you want make, but it may be necessary. If you aren't focused on the financial details of your business, however, you might not recognize the instances when it does become a necessity.

A failure to look at the right financial data can lead to your business failure. Consider the number of companies I've discussed thus far that were generating revenue but failed to recognize signs their company was dying. Business leaders can spin financial data to make things look good when in reality the business is on life support.

Here are a few of the numbers you should measure and become intimate with:

- Number of active and repeat customers
- Conversion rates

- Customer acquisition costs
- Average revenue per customer
- Lifetime value
- Churn
- Referrals
- Cash and cash flow
- Web traffic analytics
- Inventory turns
- Profit
- Customer concentration
- Internal costs
- Net performance score (NPS)

The Wheel of Profit

To analyze your revenue streams, create a profit wheel. Color in each product in terms of percentage of sales, and then look at the profitability. Is your team spending most of its time promoting a low-margin product when one with higher profitability makes up a small percentage of sales? (In addition to this profit analysis, go back and review the time tracking I discussed in Chapter 7, "The Process Edge." If the low-margin product is eating up too much time to permit your team to concentrate on the more profitable products, that should figure into the equation as well.)

Can you lower the cost structure of the product with slim margins? Will the market bear a price increase for your low-margin product, or is it a commodity that requires you to compete on price? What would it take to shift the focus to the higher-margin products? Is the market for that product sufficient to sustain your business? Finally, what threats and risks do you see for the low-margin product that could result in an even greater profitability squeeze?

Before you decide to cut a low-margin product or service, consider ways you could improve the results. Could technology make it more cost effective to deliver the product? Is there a way to auto-mate some of the work involved in producing the product or service to lower costs? As I noted in the previous chapter, technology is helping many industries where profit margins are being squeezed to increase their profitability.

Have you considered your distribution process? If you're selling directly to the client via sales representatives or a brick-and-mortar store, could you move the sales to an e-commerce platform? Many brands, such as Costco and Staples, have online exclusives—products that are available via the Internet only. That reduces the amount of inventory they have to carry in their stores, which im-proves profit margins.

Any company can use third-party fulfillment firms—Fulfillment by Amazon being one of the most popular—and/or drop shipping to realize savings and sell products that would otherwise be impos-sible to offer to their customers.

Many larger companies segment their customer base by the size of the account. Smaller customers may have online access for sup-port or a call center, whereas larger enterprises get a personal rep-resentative who attends to their needs. Such a structure allows you to keep less-profitable business without jeopardizing service to the lucrative accounts.

If you're selling through sales representatives, either as employees or independent contractors, and you pay a commission, you may need to look at your payment structure. It could be easier to sell the low-margin product rather than the higher-profit one. So incen-tivize them more to sell the higher-margin item.

Can you raise your price? Obviously an increase in pricing would help alleviate a margin squeeze, but if you lose business then it could be a wash, or even worse, a loss. Does your product offering enable you to compete on price? If not, could you reposition it to provide an additional value proposition that would justify a price increase?

When was the last time you reviewed your vendors' pricing? If you haven't renegotiated contracts in a while, now could be a good time to review. Often vendors have new, more-affordable pricing structures that you don't know about because you were already operating under the old pricing. Additionally, if the volume of your purchases has increased, you should be eligible for a volume discount.

Can you upsell your customer? I use several cloud-based services that are either free or have a low-cost entry-level price structure. However, to get the bells and whistles, you need to subscribe to the premium product.

Think about the way Amazon uses algorithms to sell more products. When you order something online with the company, before you check out, it shows you additional items that other people have purchased when making the same selection. Vistaprint is another company that is masterful at the upsell. The last two times I ordered business cards, I ended up buying additional items like a coffee mug imprinted with my logo.

If none of these suggestions will work, it's time to consider whether to cut the dead weight. That decision can't be made in a vacuum. There may be good reasons to hang onto the product. At McDonald's, for example, hamburgers are a low-margin item, and French fries have a much higher profitability. However, McDonald's couldn't cut the hamburger from its menu. It wouldn't make sense to the business.

Companies lose their footing when they use funds from a profitable market segment to shore up a losing market segment. Certainly, if it's a new area of business, then that is justifiable for a time; however, you should decide on a cut-off point. That's why the One-Percent Edge process requires constant evaluation. When you set your plan, you determine how you are going to measure your success. Regular, timely reviews of your goals and objectives will keep you poised to make adjustments as needed or let you know if it's time to pursue another strategy. Always keep in mind: Don't throw good money after bad.

With that said, I learned early in my career that making dramatic cuts in your business won't propel it into prosperity. It might enhance your bottom line, but it isn't a long-term, innovative solution to growth. Let's face it, there's only so much fat you can trim from a budget. Plus, innovative companies should be investing in enhancements and improvements. If your resources are cut down to the bone, you won't have the bandwidth to seize new opportunities.

The Point of Diminishing Returns

I've worked with companies where growth goals were established and managers knew they had to achieve those goals by whatever means it took. They emphasized top-line growth even as the companies' bottom lines fell. Growth for the sake of growth doesn't ensure your sustainability and continued relevance. Companies should be wary of pushing growth by expanding locations and/or acquiring other businesses past the point of diminishing returns.

High performance companies rely on operational improvements to drive increased sales within existing parameters. In other words, they increase revenues by lowering expenses. Sounds simple enough, doesn't it? But unfortunately, many business leaders lose sight of this as they chase top-line growth. Eventually it catches up with them, and the business implodes.

With the One-Percent Edge process you must review your current sales and productivity and determine why growth is stalling or declining before you make major decisions to push growth by other methods. Are there new products you can introduce to enhance revenue? Are you too heavily staffed? Are there ways to automate services?

Market Cannibalization

First, let me explain what cannibalization is from my perspective. Generally, it refers to the idea that a new product at a lower price eats into the market share of a current product with a higher price. As a growth strategy, organizations often introduce new products that ultimately compete with existing ones. In other words, they compete against themselves. This strategy can be effective, but the financial metrics must be carefully monitored and measured. The risk is that the new lower-priced offering may drag down pricing of other products, reducing overall profitability.

The leaders of Kodak were afraid to introduce digital photography for fear it would cannibalize its more profitable core business. By the time they decided to enter the market, it was too late. Similarly Bausch & Lomb invented the soft contact lens but failed to launch it because the firm did not want to lose the lucrative business of selling the drops that hard lenses require. As a result, Johnson & Johnson swept into soft lenses, and the market for hard lenses disappeared.

When you see an opportunity for a new, lower-priced product that's the right fit for your market, you should seriously consider it. If you don't seize the opportunity, a competitor or a lean start-up most likely will.

When faced with this dilemma, take into consideration the size of your market and your product's market share. Also, think about your product's average sales price and its gross margin. Then estimate the gross margin for your new product and its approximate share of the market. How much of that business will be derived from your current, higher-paying customer base? If your new product is reaching a different type of customer than your current offering, then your risk is minimal. However, if your estimates demonstrate that the new product could seriously affect the sales of your current business, it may not be a wise decision.

Keep in mind as you analyze such opportunities that the goal is profitable growth, not just more sales. Shrinkage of your profitable product offering and lower profit margins overall can mean the demise of your business.

Understand Your Maximum Capacity

Quite a few years ago, a business owner developed a trash-bag product that looked like a pumpkin. It was perfect for the fall near Halloween, when many homeowners are raking up bags of leaves and placing them on the curb for trash pickup. Shortly after he introduced the product, Walmart picked it up. An exciting moment for sure until he couldn't meet the sales demand and the business fizzled out.

Knowing your maximum capacity is important for your planning, sales team, and customer experience. Shortly before the holidays last year, I purchased an Amazon Echo. I loved it and decided to buy a couple as gifts for family members. However, when I tried to order them, I learned that the merchandise wouldn't be available until the end of January or the beginning of February. Major brands such as Apple or Amazon may be able to survive the inability to fulfill a customer's order because they have unique and innovative products, but a small-to-midsize business can't. Your customers will go elsewhere.

For a service business, when you take on new clients and customers, it's important you have the capacity to service them. However, it's tempting to take on as much business as you can without thinking through your resources. I've worked with people who are constantly making excuses for missing deadlines. It seems the only time you get their attention is when you complain about the lack of service.

This makes measuring your maximum capacity and keeping a close eye on it an important metric for you to understand as you grow your company.

Turning Excess Capacity into Revenue Opportunities

If your business is product driven, excess capacity occurs when your output is less than optimal, resulting from a lack of a demand. For a service business, it means you have downtime because your team has more time than you have business. Some companies use excess capacity to offer customers special promotions and generate more sales near the end of the month. I've seen many companies use this approach to move inventory via platforms such as Groupon.

Uber has an interesting way to use excess capacity. Drivers can't be occupied transporting people all the time, so in 2015, the company launched UberEATS, a standalone platform for ordering meals from local restaurants.

A printing company might subcontract jobs from a competitor instead of letting its presses sit idle. Excess office space can be rented out to another business to help offset costs. Even your equipment that sits idle could be shared with another company as a way to leverage the asset.

As a speaker, I have excess capacity because I'm not booked every day of the week. My friend, Keith Alper, founded a company called Geniecast (full disclosure: I am an investor in the company). Its mission is to transform the way the world connects people, ideas, and inspiration. Geniecast has an impressive menu of thought leaders and subject-matter experts who can be booked to appear at an event via its interactive, two-way video broadcast platform. For example, I was booked to speak at the Texas governor's conference on small business. Using the Geniecast technology, I was able to speak to the group from my home and still interact well with the entire audience. Speakers accept a reduced fee, but they don't have to travel, and it absorbs some of the excess capacity. The company's tagline is "Anyone. Anywhere. Anytime."

How can your company monetize its excess capacity to increase top- and bottom-line results?

Not All Sales Are Good Sales

Every business needs to make sales. However, not all sales are good sales. Growth for growth's sake doesn't automatically ensure sustainability. Becoming intimate with the numbers driving your business gives you the ability to weigh growth decisions against the company's resources and capacity. Growing too fast can quickly sink your ship if you aren't equipped to handle it, or if the sales are not priced correctly or sold to the right type of customer.

Cash Is King

Amazon's ability to generate cash makes the U.S. Mint jealous. How is your business doing in this regard? If it seems to you like you're doing well, but you're having problems making payroll or keeping up with your accounts payable, you need to take a serious look at your cash flow. It's an area where even good businesses can improve.

Here is a metric that will help you gauge where you stand today. It will also help you target the areas where you need to improve.

The ability of your business to generate cash is captured in something called the cash conversion cycle (CCC). The formula for the CCC is three basic steps:

1. Start with the number of days of inventory you have on hand.
2. Add how long it takes customers to pay you.
3. Subtract how many days it takes you to pay your suppliers.

When this number is low, it means you have a good cash flow. You won't believe what Amazon's CCC number was recently. (I'll share that in just a few moments). If you consider that formula, you'll see that it's a bad thing to have a lot of cash tied up in inventory and accounts receivable and that it's a good thing to delay paying your bills for as long as possible—not rocket science, but important to know and control.

How low can you go?

Writing on this topic for *Harvard Business Review*, Justin Fox said that efficient retailers like Walmart and Costco have CCCs in the single digits. That's nothing compared to Amazon, which had a CCC of negative 30.6 days back in 2013. Apple is another star, scoring a negative 44.5. In other words, they don't carry much inventory, they get paid with lightning speed, and they are able to hold off their creditors rather well.

This is a simple formula to remember and use in your business. But aside from measuring cold hard cash, it's more important to consider it as a measurement of how well you are managing your business.

Frankly, sales are not always completely in your control, but in general, every element in the CCC formula is. You should be able to control your inventory, how long you're kept waiting for payment, and how long you're able to stretch out payments to your supplier.

Your goal should be to drive down your CCC as far as possible. Further, always keep your eye on it. It's easy to let some of these elements slide. If you take your eyes off these metrics, inventory can build up, and client payments can slip. Suddenly, you're in a cash-flow crunch.

This analysis applies to service businesses as well. I said it earlier, and it's true: Sometimes you need to walk away or even fire a client in order to manage your finances and the growth of your organization. To build a sustainable company, there are times when less is more. You should recognize those times.

Too frequently, business owners and business leaders lower their prices with the hope of generating more sales. However, while their top line may increase, the company's bottom line may decrease significantly. Service businesses often fall victim to this low-price scenario because they don't have a retail product to sell. However, in a service business, it's not just about your cost of goods, but about the soft costs too, such as your time.

I used to go shopping at Macy's with an armload of coupons and feel as though they almost paid me to take items out of the store. By the time I purchased items on sale and used my coupons, the merchandise was almost free. It didn't help Macy's or build loyalty. In my case, I waited to make purchases until I had enough coupons. As you probably know, Macy's announced in 2016 it was shuttering hundreds of stores. The company's new CEO has been quoted as stating he will discontinue the massive couponing on clearance items and instead position all clearance merchandise marked with the final price in one area of the store called the "Last Act." Has Macy's brand been tarnished in the market? How will customers respond to the changes? Without the coupons, will customers go elsewhere?

Similar problems have occurred when businesses use loss-leader deals to get customers in the door with companies such as Groupon. The special promotion/deal may result in a spike in sales, but it doesn't mean those customers will ever return. Price integrity and engagement build repeat business.

Price Appropriately

The One-Percent Edge requires you to define your unique value in terms of your product/service. When your business value is clearly defined, there is no need to cut prices. Your customers will pay the price because they know they can't get your offering anywhere else. If you begin competing on price, you'll lose your edge in the market.

To get a perspective on pricing, let's first take an imaginary stroll through the aisles of two retailers, Walmart and Saks Fifth Avenue. Both are leaders in their markets. What follows isn't a criticism of either one. We're taking this stroll to observe human behavior and psychology when it comes to value.

If we walk through Walmart at almost any time of day, we'll see a lot of people shopping, but if we hang out long enough and are observant enough, we're going to notice a few abandoned shopping carts as well as some clothing that has been picked up as if to buy but set aside randomly throughout the store.

The folks at Walmart do a pretty good job of picking up these discards, but they happen.

If we do a similar stroll through Saks, we'll find that they don't have shopping carts, but that's not really the point. What we're looking for is clothing that has been picked up with the intention of buying it, but the customer changed her mind and carelessly tossed it aside. Did you find any abandoned purchases in Saks? Me neither.

The point I want to make is that psychologically, it's much more difficult for people to abandon a high-value item after they have taken the initial steps to buy it. Smaller purchases are more inconsequential; we really don't have a problem of saying "never mind" and moving on. Inexpensive items don't have the same connection to our hearts and minds.

This is important to understand when you set your pricing. Higher-priced items deliver a greater perceived value to customers. As a result, it's difficult to turn our backs on adding significant value to our lives, both personally and professionally. Often you'll hear a higher-priced product or service referred to as an "investment" as opposed to a "purchase." If you consider buying a training program that costs several thousand dollars, you're looking at an investment in your success. But if you sign up for a seminar or webinar for $35, it's no big deal if you don't show up. The same even applies to clothing purchases at high-end retailers; it's called investment dressing.

Does that sound counterintuitive to you? Think about it this way: A business owner without the One-Percent Edge wants to increase revenue, so she decides to discount her pricing to attract more customers or clients. She begins to spread the word via social media or email marketing. She hands out coupons, and maybe even signs up for a deal-of-the-day coupon company such as Groupon. In the short term, her strategy may work. She may see a slight increase in sales, but when this discount sale is over, the customers will be gone.

Competing on price is not a sustainable business strategy because generally there is always someone who is willing to provide the same product or service at an even lower price. I've mentioned a friend who was involved in selling books over the Internet in the early days of e-commerce. He worked hard to put efficiencies in place that allowed the company to sell recently published books at very slim margins. That pushed the company into the black.

However, he woke up one morning to discover that a competitor with deeper pockets had started selling recently published books below cost. That pushed his company back into the red. Competing on price alone often leads to a war of attrition.

There's another downside to offering bargain-basement prices: You risk being viewed as a "cheap" outfit rather than a company known for high-quality products or services that deliver real value to the buyer. The only customers you'll land are those who are constantly on the hunt for the lowest possible price. You simply can't build lasting relationships with these consumers. The price of their loyalty is nothing more than a few bucks of savings.

Kmart and Walmart were both founded in 1962, but their stories are very different. While Kmart started off strong, Walmart ultimately became the leading discounter in the market. Kmart continued to try to compete with Walmart on price alone, and that strategy landed it in bankruptcy in 2002. "Without a clear way to play, and capabilities to support it, a company cannot achieve the coherence it needs to truly excel at what it does, and thus outpace competitors," notes Paul Leinwand, a Partner in Booz & Company.[1]

On the other hand, the other major discounter, Target, successfully differentiated itself from Walmart by defining its own niche. Target gives customers a slightly more upscale experience while still offering low prices that are competitive with Walmart's everyday low prices. Kudos to Target for being able to carve out a profitable niche in a very competitive industry.

The smartphone battle between Samsung and Apple is another good case study. If you just scan the business or technology page (or blog) headlines, you would believe that Apple is getting its digital lunch handed to it by Samsung:

- "Samsung continues to rule over Apple in the smartphone market." —CNET
- "Samsung widens gap over Apple in world smartphone market." —MACRUMORS
- "Samsung again easily sells more phones than Apple in Q4." —FAST COMPANY

But that's just part of the story, and probably not the most important part. A *Wired* headline tells us what's important: "Apple Doesn't Sell All the Phones. But It Makes All the Money." Apple reigns supreme over the premium side of the smartphone market; compared to Samsung, it enjoys a much wider profit margin per phone.[2]

Samsung can watch its unit sales skyrocket and still never find itself in the enviable position where Apple sits. Its challenge is to find a way to take a larger share of the upscale market. If Samsung were manufacturing phones in a high-labor-cost area, it could, of course, make some headway by shifting its operation. But I assume, as an Asian company, it's already doing what it can in this area. This brings us to strategies that allow you to put your labor costs in a stronger financial footing.

Financial Benefits of Outsourcing

Outsourcing all kinds of labor costs, both direct and indirect, is easier today than it has ever been. If you're a manufacturer, you probably have some knowledge of setting up shop or contracting for work in China and other locations. However, the Internet has created the ability to contract for all kinds of talent at a lower cost than what you are probably paying for work you're doing in-house.

Your first task is to find the areas where you can leverage these lower costs. Data entry, spreadsheet creation, social media posting, scheduling, writing, graphic arts, research, translation, website management, administrative tasks, customer service, legal services, data analytics, and software development are among the skills commonly acquired via online contract relationships. Usually the low-cost contract workers are located offshore. The Philippines, for example, has emerged in recent years as a great source for "virtual assistants."

Do you have a sense for how the skills cross over with the tasks your employees are currently performing for you? Even if you think you have a handle on it, you should have your team do some time tracking to find the best opportunities for outsourcing.

But here's an extremely important principle: Don't outsource for the sake of outsourcing. You need to have a goal in mind. You may want to lower your payroll as a percentage of your finances. In that case, you'll need to spend some time establishing the right relationships with freelancers and other outsource service providers and then scale it up as you gain confidence. At some point, through reductions in staff or growth in your overall business, you will want to see concrete numbers. You need to set a goal for a percentage reduction in overhead payroll costs, for example, and be vigilant about measuring your progress against that goal.

Outsourcing to Combat Lost Opportunities

The important outcome, as I just outlined, is to reduce payroll costs as a percentage of your business. This can be just as easily accomplished by growing the business as by laying off employees. But there is one important stumbling block you need to be aware of.

Your in-house team should be your high-value players. When you have them audit their time, attach values to the various tasks they perform. Some of these will have significantly lower values than others. Your goal with outsourcing is to assign those lower-value tasks to a lower-priced contract worker. However, the end result cannot be to merely lighten the load for the higher-value local members of your team. You'll need to have higher-value tasks for them to perform to replace the time spent doing the tasks you off-load to contract workers.

Therefore, at the same time you identify the low-value tasks that you want to move offshore, you need to identify higher-value tasks to fill the void you are creating locally. If you can't find better ways to invest the time of your local team, then hiring offshore contract workers will have the opposite result from your intended outcome: You'll merely be adding another labor expense to your overhead.

A quick injection of revenue may sound appealing today, but you need to think about the long-term consequences to your brand. Rather than succumbing to a short-term fix, focus on creating real value for your customers. Give them something they can't get anywhere else.

Build an exclusive offering. If customers want X, Y, and Z, then your business is the place to go. Otherwise, they have to settle for something less. And keep in mind customers will pay the price for something they truly want and value.

The One-Percent Pricing Factor

Companies consistently undercharge for their products despite spending millions or even billions of dollars to develop or acquire them. Consider this: What if you raised your prices by only 1 percent? You wouldn't incur any additional operating costs other than an incremental increase in taxes, so the additional dollars would go directly to your bottom line. The increase in profit depends on the size of your business. You can easily do the math to determine what a 1 percent revenue increase would amount to, then subtract the taxes and you'll have the number that will hit your bottom line. Now, what could your business do with the additional revenue?

There can be good reasons to set a low price: You want to get established in a new market, increase market share, or you're in a commodity market. However, be absolutely sure you aren't throwing away value. The math is unforgiving. If you miss your optimum price by just 1 percent, it can make nearly a 10-percent difference in profits, according to a McKinsey & Company analysis of S&P 1500 companies.[3]

There are various ways to increase pricing in your business. First, you can just start increasing prices across the board. Don't be afraid to do it. A couple I know owned a small inn. The husband was always reluctant to boost prices. The wife wasn't, and she usually won the arguments. The husband soon became a believer, however, because they never lost business with a price increase.

You can maximize revenue if you consider these points and use them to influence your pricing decisions:

- What consumers know about your pricing
- Your relative pricing position versus the competition
- Your features versus the competition
- The various segments of your market, including niche consumers

The Price Is Right

When you clearly define the value your product or service brings to the market you'll be better equipped to find the right price. You need to analyze your pricing outside the framework of your internal perceptions. You may know that your product will reduce costs for the end user by 25 percent, which establishes a starting point for your pricing analysis. However, it would be far more valuable and insightful to ask open-ended questions of your customers to understand how they perceive the value and what price they are willing to pay for that value.

Customer Profitability

You may remember I recommended creating a product profit wheel for your business. You also need a customer profitability review, but there is a problem with acquiring that information. Most traditional accounting systems report product gross profit margins. Therefore, managers can't see the equally important and relevant customer-related expenses such as distribution channel, selling, customer service, credit, and marketing expenses. Your marketing and sales teams may already intuitively sense which customers are less profitable, but they lack the quantitative evidence to support their positions.

Staying relevant in your industry means not simply making sales but making profitable sales to the right customers. Your accounting systems may use an average profitability by customer. Viewed from that perspective, your business could look healthy. However, there may be customers who are costing you money.

If you aren't already getting this information from your financial department, you should request it. With this information you may be able to create a tiered approach to your customer base.

Less-profitable customers receive a lower level of service versus higher-profit customers.

Don't Leave Money on the Table

My mother always told me that when negotiating to purchase something or to sell something, if the other party says yes at the opening offer, you've left money on the table. According to a McKinsey & Company report, companies frequently leave money on the table when it comes to introducing new products to the market.[4] So let's take a look at where you should go once you've diversified your revenue streams.

Using the Wrong Pricing Systems?

Too often companies use either a cost-plus system or an incremental system to set the prices of new products. With an incremental system, you would look at last year's model and bump up the price a bit on the new and improved model. However, if this year's entry really is new and improved, how much will consumers value those improvements? It's easy to undervalue a product either because you're too close to the situation and blind to the bigger picture or because you're in the grip of competitive fears.

Create and Recognize Value

Value-based pricing has the power to dramatically increase your bottom line. It should also influence how you develop new products and services. But a good value-based pricing structure is more difficult to build when compared to the incremental or cost-plus approaches. The problem is that you have to measure buyer perception.

For example, if you provide an automation solution that allows a manufacturer to speed up an assembly line by 10 percent, would that only warrant a 10-percent price increase over current technology, or is that more valuable to the manufacturer? In this case, perhaps the time saved offers the end user a new opportunity, so the full benefit is a decrease in operational cost plus revenue from a new venture.

The Death of the Quarterly Report: Key Performance Indicators

Sophisticated fighter jets—and now even some expensive automobiles—offer a "heads up" dashboard display. It enables pilots and drivers to look out the windshield and still see all their crucial gauges.

In the same way, you should have a dashboard of key performance indicators (KPIs) that you can see while you're in the trenches running your business every day.

Well, almost every day, and that brings us to an important point: Don't wait for quarterly reports. Your KPI dashboard should be available to you at least on a monthly basis, and in many cases weekly, biweekly, or even daily would be better. With the accounting and inventory-control software available today, this should be possible. If you only see these figures on a quarterly basis, you'll always be navigating by squinting into your rearview mirror.

One of the foundational principles of quality assurance—if you can't measure it, you can't control it—applies to business in general. Be sure you can accurately generate all the important metrics required to understand where your business stands. Without that information, or with incorrect information, you will make bad decisions.

Now let's list some KPIs to help you measure, control, and improve your growth:

▶ **Lifetime value (LTV).** You need to know how much your customer is worth to your business. This is going to help you with various decisions you'll need to make.

▶ **Customer retention and customer attrition.** How long are you keeping your customers? Always take at least two snapshots of this figure, at thirty days and at ninety days. When customers seemingly fall out at thirty days, how often do they come back within ninety days?

▶ **Customer acquisition cost.** How much does it cost your business to get a new customer? Compare it to LTV. If your acquisition cost is near to or greater than your LTV, you need to go back to the drawing board. Also, what's your customer retention cost? What works to maintain customer loyalty?

▶ **Sales or revenue by category, product, or service.** Here's one you need to monitor as closely as possible in real time. Understanding what's selling and what isn't allows you to better control inventory, find opportunities to bump up prices, and know when it's time to have a fire sale.

▶ **Your growth versus your industry's growth.** Are you on par, lagging, or leading your competitors in growth? You may be happy with 3-percent yearly growth. But if everyone else is doing 5 percent, you're going to have a hard time selling your business when the day comes. Plus, it may be a good indication that something is awry in your company.

As you're keeping track of earnings before interest, taxes, depreciation, and amortization, keep your head up and your eyes open, and watch these KPIs too.

Determining Customer Value

Because I work with businesses of all sizes, I get to peer into their internal analyses. I'm not surprised when smaller firms don't know how to determine customer value, but some of the major brands with which I work can't answer the questions either. Understanding the value of your customers is critical for agile decision making.

There are two numbers you have to balance properly if you want to assure long-term success:

- The cost of acquiring a customer (CAC)
- The customer's lifetime value (LTV)

As I said earlier, if the cost of acquiring a customer is greater than that customer's lifetime value, you're in big trouble. Yes, that's obvious, but the story's not quite that simple. If you're a start-up or for some other reason don't have adequate financial data (sales and marketing)—maybe your record keeping isn't good enough—you're operating in the dark.

Estimating these numbers as a start-up is a necessity, but once you begin marketing, buying merchandise, and making sales, you must have a solid system in place that captures and properly categorizes your income and your expenses. If you do that, it puts you in a position to correctly calculate CAC and LTV. With those numbers you can make smart decisions going forward. Let's see how those two vital indicators are calculated.

Formula for CAC

CAC is simply all the costs—sales and marketing basically—that go into acquiring a new customer over a given period of time. If you spend $100 in one month to acquire 100 new customers in one month, your CAC is $1.

This is pretty straightforward once your business gets rolling. However, there can be times when it gets bumped out of whack. For example, if you're starting a new business, you may pump extra money into marketing in the beginning and be in a position to throttle back a little when you're better established.

Formula for LTV

As noted in Chapter 3, the simplest formula for how to work out LTV is to multiply three numbers: the value (net profit) of each sale to a customer, the number of sales made to a customer in a year, and the number of years a customer remains a customer (if a customer drops out sooner than one year, this would be a fraction). The formula is:

$$\text{LTV} = (\text{value of a sale}) \times (\text{number of sales}) \times (\text{life of customer in years})$$

If your CAC roughly equals your LTV, your marketing efforts are not paying off. Having information like this tells you that you need to:

- **Increase LTV:** upsell, raise prices, offer bigger-ticket items, and lengthen the life of a customer
- **Cut or optimize your marketing budget:** automate, segment better, find the right channels, etc.
- **Do both of the above**

LTV Modeling for Decision Making

Once you have good historic numbers for your CAC and LTV models, you can look for opportunities. Running at an LTV-to-CAC ratio of 3–1 is generally considered good. (Ultimately you'll need to determine the LTV best for your business.) If you find yourself in a position where you're doing even better than that, you may want to consider taking some of that extra money you're making and plowing it back into your business to grow your customer base.

The other side of the coin is that if you notice your ratio slipping, it gives you a good early warning sign that something may be hurting your business. It could be that your product or service is getting outdated and customers are dropping away at a faster pace than before.

If you have good numbers for your CAC and LTV you are in a much stronger position to understand what's happening in your business and make the midcourse corrections necessary to keep it strong.

Net Performance Score (NPS)

NPS is a management tool that allows business leaders to measure customer loyalty. Well over half of the Fortune 1000 companies use this measurement. The score is derived from asking a customer one simple question: How likely is it that you would recommend our company/product/service to a friend or colleague? Respondents answer on a scale of zero to ten, with zero being highly unlikely and ten being highly likely.

Customers who respond with a nine or ten rating are considered promoters for your business. It's generally believed that these customers will buy more, stay with you longer, and refer additional business to you. Those customers who respond with a zero or one are known as detractors. Those responding with a seven or eight are considered passives. The NPS is then calculated by subtracting the number of detractors from the number of promoters. Passives are included in the final scoring for a weighted average.

Companies often include an open-ended question to allow customers to elaborate on their rating. Once identified, promoters should be given more personalized attention because these are your drivers of growth. Additionally, positive remarks should be forwarded to front-line employees as evidence of their good work. Negative comments may be used to turn detractors into loyal fans. For example, I completed one of these quick surveys after having a terrible experience with a major brand. Within a few days a customer service representative called me to resolve the issue. The matter was cleared up, and I remained a customer.

Businesses of all sizes should be able to track and review their NPS on a regular basis with relative ease. You can track the NPS for your brand as a whole or by product, customer segment, or geographic areas. Consider the NPS analysis as your company's customer balance sheet. The goal is for the number of your supporters to be significantly greater than the number of your detractors

Large brands may use sophisticated software programs or outsource the NPS analysis to another company. If you are leading a smaller organization, don't despair. Online survey tools can help you get a good sense of where your company stands with your customers. If you're not comfortable calculating the score yourself, there are free calculators online such as the one at http://www.npscalculator.com/en.

Investing in Talent

Finding the right talent to create a business with the One-Percent Edge is critical, as I discussed in Chapter 5, "The People Edge." Companies that do the best job at managing their talent enjoy the greatest success. However, there is a scramble to find good talent in today's market. Plus, employees tend to be less loyal than they were in the past. There is a documented skills gap in the United States. Therefore, companies of all sizes tend to bring people on board who might not be top performers. Small businesses make this mistake more frequently than larger firms that have more money and attractive benefit packages.

From a financial perspective, here is the reality about investing in the right talent: According to a McKinsey & Company study, senior managers have found that "A players"—the best 20 percent or so of managers—raise operational productivity, profit, and sales revenue much more than average performers. While A players demand a higher pay rate, the researchers noted paying an additional 40 percent to hire an A player could yield an overall return of 100 percent or more in a single year. Tolerating underperformers costs your company real dollars.[5]

Customer Concentration

The adage "Don't put all your eggs in one basket" holds true on every day of the year except Easter. Take this advice seriously, especially in this digital age when product life cycles and customer sensibilities change more quickly than the leaves in Vermont come October. Sadly, I've seen companies fold because their leaders didn't pay attention to the customer concentration metric. If a significant percentage of your business is coming from one customer, that's a serious red flag. It is also a failing that can significantly lower the value of your business when you decide it's time to sell.

Go back to your profit wheel and take a look at your product mix. Listen to what it's telling you. Is one revenue stream your only ace in the hole? Think about your investment portfolio. You wouldn't put your entire nest egg into one stock. That would be stupid. The same is true for your business (review Chapter 4, "The Product Edge"). A diversified revenue stream allows you to weather the market's ups and downs. If one customer segment or product begins to lose ground, your business will be able to reposition and sustain itself.

Hollywood Video and Blockbuster put all their eggs in the local video rental business. The former is completely gone and the latter, well, it's pretty much gone too. You don't want that to happen to your business. Part of the answer is diversification, but it's an answer that is much more easily offered than implemented. You need to strap on your thinking cap for this one and tap the most creative minds in your business.

First, identify new customer opportunities. Add features that will make your product or service appealing to a different group of consumers. Springer Equipment sells forklifts. Recognizing a market for salvaged forklift parts, the company began to disassemble gear in its boneyard and add the spare parts to its parts-department inventory.

Here are a few more ideas for concentrating your customers:

► **Find related products.** Are there products or services that go along with what you sell? Perhaps there are training materials that you can offer as well. A medical equipment company, for example, found a new niche in providing ongoing training and support for its equipment. The most aggressive version of this strategy is to buy a company that makes products related to yours. If you can swing it, this can be a smart move. You diversify your lineup and remove a potential competitor from the playing field. We've seen that a lot lately with companies such as Facebook and Amazon.

► **Offer an integrated solution.** This flows from the previous idea, and the basic question you need to ask yourself and your team is, "Can we do more?" This might be anything: training, cloud services, apps, additional gear, monitoring, servicing—the possibilities are endless.

► **Find out what's next.** Are technological changes beginning to erode your base? Don't be the last in your industry to sense where things are going. Devote part of your business to meeting the needs of the early adopters and you'll be ready if a major shift occurs. (Remember the earlier story about Kodak burying its head in the sand with digital photography and failing to realize that it wasn't in the photo print business but the story-telling business.)

▶ **Sell online.** If you don't offer your products over the Internet, add an e-commerce element to your website and diversify your sales channels. If you already sell online, sell online more. Look at the various marketplace programs that major e-tailers like Amazon have. Consider opening an eBay store, especially if you have miscellaneous overstock items in your warehouse. Rather than marking them down to next to nothing and under-cutting new products, sell them on eBay.

▶ **Open another location.** If you're exclusively online, consider diversifying your sales channels by opening a physical location. If you have one physical location, should you open a second?

▶ **Go overseas.** Not every business has the wherewithal to launch an overseas operation. Right now the big players are eyeing Africa the way they eyed Asia a decade ago. Network in your community and see if any businesses are exploring overseas ventures. You may find a project where your company's a fit. Rather than taking excessive markdowns for your overstock or outdated inventory, you should find alternative sales channels. Selling overseas can be the ideal way to move items like these, and often at reasonable prices.

▶ **Follow the growth.** If you're located in an area with disheart-ening demographics or punishing tax rates, see if you should expand to a lower tax growth area. Look at the South, Texas, and North Dakota. Would one of these areas be a good candi-date for a branch office?

Don't Play Favorites

Have you determined how much "business" one department in your company is doing with another department?

You have several functions that you consider your overhead, but to which departments, groups, or individuals should most of that overhead be charged? That's an important question to ask, especially when you begin to grow, launch new endeavors, and acquire other companies.

We know that Google and other high-tech ventures are famous for gobbling up smaller companies they think may someday be useful to their core business or represent a promising new area of commerce. However, it's easy to fall into a trap where you think something like, "Well, we already have the HR, PR, and legal teams to support this. We can add the new venture to the fold without incurring a lot of new overhead expenses."

Ruth Porat, CFO of Alphabet Inc. (Google's parent company), had to do some major cutting because she discovered that many of Google's projects and acquisitions weren't being charged for much of their overhead costs. They were taking a free ride from Google's cash-generating core businesses. Porat began to hold those businesses accountable for their costs as if they were independent start-ups.

This is a common problem. Business leaders tend to fall madly in love with their new projects—and then the shine goes off the older segments of their businesses. Owners and managers can be irrational when evaluating the costs of their brand-new toys, hoping that in the long run their wishes will come true.

The problem might not stop there. The love affair with the new venture causes leadership to lose focus on the core business, causing it to suffer. It doesn't help that the legacy operation is being stretched to the limit working to provide overhead and support for the new project.

Don't make decisions based on emotion. The financial facts of your business will not yield to your emotional desires.

CONCLUSION

A Company with the One-Percent Edge

I hope you're convinced by now that it is inevitable that all companies, no matter how mighty, will at some point find it necessary to reinvent themselves to varying degrees in order to remain relevant in today's changing market. The consequences are significant for business leaders who fail to recognize this and establish a process to make innovation a part of their organization's DNA. When your business reaches a point where growth is difficult and your market is diminished, it's most often too late to pivot and position yourself for survival.

Remember your high school biology class? At some point you probably watched a video that showed cells reproducing. What starts out as one cell is suddenly two cells, which morph into four, and so on. Each cell does its job by creating a new cell, and the organism as a whole gets bigger and stronger over time. The important part, however, is that each cell, by virtue of its identical DNA, is predictably guiding the entire organism toward a common goal.

This is a good picture of an organic business organization on a steady road to growth. Every employee in the company shares the same organizational DNA. Geneticists often call DNA a roadmap. The One-Percent Edge process is a roadmap for success. When it's instilled in all the members of your team, it becomes the organization's DNA. If you have good, healthy DNA, growth starts to happen naturally.

Take a moment and use this imagery to consider the challenges your company faces. In every chapter of this book, I've described business successes and failures. When human DNA is damaged, cancer is one of the terrible outcomes. The same applies to your business: If you allow damaged DNA to get a foothold, there will eventually be one or more cancers in your organization, something no business can afford today.

Think of the One-Percent Edge process as your safeguard against damaged DNA.

Competition is fierce, and maintaining the edge will help you stay ahead of the curve. Instead of reacting to changes, you'll be in a better position to predict them. However, a competitive advantage is fleeting.

I hope your primary takeaway from this book is that your relationship with your customers is the one sustainable advantage that insulates your business against failure. Of course, that means every aspect of your organization must support that relationship and consistently deliver it to the market. It means you are constantly listening to your customers' needs as a problem solver and partner, and enhancing your business operations to provide solutions in a profitable and productive way.

The One-Percent Edge is the result of a disciplined process to identify opportunities and strategies, prioritize them, plan for them, execute, measure, adjust or abandon, and repeat.

As President Dwight Eisenhower once said, "In preparing for battle I have always found that plans are useless but planning is indispensable."

NOTES

INTRODUCTION

1. Michael Bergdahl, *The 10 Rules of Sam Walton: Success Secrets for Remark-able Results* (Wiley), 2010, p. 30.
2. Friederike Fabritius, MS and Hans W. Hagermann, PhD, *The Leading Brain: Powerful Science-Based Strategies for Achieving Peak Performance* (Penguin), 2017, p. 158.

CHAPTER 1

1. Paul Hurd, "The State of Critical Thinking Today: The Need for a Substantive Concept of Critical Thinking," https://www.criticalthinking.org/resources/articles/the-state-ct-today.shtml.
2. Impro Theatre, Improvisational School & Theatre website, http://improtheatre.com/corporate-improv-benefits/.
3. Robert Half, "Creative Workspace Solutions that Make Employees Happy," September 8, 2016, https://www.roberthalf.com/creativegroup/blog/creative-workspace-solutions-that-make-employees-happy.
4. Chris Bradley, Lowell Bryan, and Sven Smit, "Managing the Strategy Journey," McKinsey & Company, July 2012, http://www.mckinsey.com/business-functions/strategy-and-corporate-finance/our-insights/managing-the-strategy-journey.
5. Libby Kane, "Why an Oscar-Winning Pixar Director Gets Nervous When Everything Is Going Right," *Business Insider*, June 1, 2016, http://www.businessinsider.com/pixar-director-andrew-stanton-gets-nervous-when-everything-goes-right-2016-6.

CHAPTER 2

1. Doug Williamson, "True Leaders Believe Dissent Is an Obligation," January 17, 2017, http://www.dougwilliamson.ca/2017/01/17/true-leaders-believe-dissent-is-an-obligation/.

CHAPTER 3

1. "Survey Reveals Half of Customers Will Select Another Competitor Within a Day of Receiving Poor Customer Service," [24]7, February 16, 2016, https://www.247-inc.com/company/press-releases/247-survey-reveals-half-customers-will-select-another-competitor-within-day.

2. Susan Solovic, "Don't Just Fix the Problem, Fix the Customer," August 16,2016,http://www.susansolovic.com/2016/08/dont-just-fix-the-problem-fix-the-customer/.
3. Thomas C. Frohlich, "Cars with the Oldest Buyers," *USA Today*, October 4, 2014, https://www.usatoday.com/story/money/cars/2014/10/04/24-7-wall-st-cars-oldest-buyers/16587437/.
4. William H. Frey, "Diversity Defines the Millennial Generation," Brookings, June 28, 2016, https://www.brookings.edu/blog/.the-avenue/2016/06/28/diversity-defines-the-millennial-generation/.
5. Anna Marie de la Fuente, "MundoFox Shuts Down News Division, Changes Name to MundoMax," *Variety*, July 31, 2015, http://variety.com/2015/tv/global/mundofox-shuts-down-news-division-now-mundomax-1201554102/.
6. "Poor Social Media Practices can Negatively Impact a Businesses' Bottom Line and Brand Image," J.D. Power, February 14, 2013, http://www.jdpower.com/press-releases/2013-social-media-benchmark-study.
7. Jay Baer, "42 Percent of Consumers Complaining in Social Media Expect 60 Minute Response Time," Convince & Convert, http://www.convinceandconvert.com/social-media-research/42-percent-of-consumers-complaining-in-social-media-expect-60-minute-response-time/.
8. Brittney Helmrich, "10 Companies That Totally Rock Customer Service on Social Media," *Business News Daily*, December 15, 2014, http://www.businessnewsdaily.com/7578-social-media-customer-service.html#sthash.Feiykh04.dpuf.
9. Scott Horn, "So Many Channels, So Little Time: Insight into the Omnichannel Journey," [24]7, June 3, 2015, https://www.247-inc.com/company/blog/so-many-channels-so-little-time-insight-omnichannel-journey.
10. Julie Jargon, "Starbucks Links 'Stars' to Bucks in Loyalty-Program Shift," *The Wall Street Journal*, February 22, 2016, https://www.wsj.com/articles/starbucks-corp-changing-its-loyalty-program-1456158689.

CHAPTER 4

1. IBM, *2015 Annual Report*, IBM, https://www.ibm.com/annualreport/2015/bin/assets/IBM-Annual-Report-2015.pdf.
2. Jay Cole, "Tesla Looked To Women When Designing The Model X," Inside EVs, 2015, http://insideevs.com/tesla-looked-to-women-when-designing-the-model-x/.
3. Stephanie Baker, "Zara's Recipe for Success: More Data, Fewer Bosses," Smartinvestor.in, November 23, 2016, http://smartinvestor.business-standard.com/market/.
4. Sharon Terlep, "Gillette, Bleeding Market Share, Cuts Prices of Razors," *Wall Street Journal*, April 4, 2017, https://www.wsj.com/articles/.gillette-bleeding-market-share-cuts-prices-of-razors-1491303601.

5. Susan Solovic, "What You Can Learn from the Startup that Pulled Piano Lessons into the Internet Age," Greenwich Time, January 20, 2016, http://www.greenwichtime.com/news/article/What-You-Can-Learn-from-the-Startup-that-Pulled-6772180.php.

6. James H. Gilmore and B. Joseph Pine II, "The Four Faces of Mass Customization," *Harvard Business Review*, January-February 1997, https://hbr.org/1997/01/the-four-faces-of-mass-customization.

7. International Trade Administration, "Exporting Is Good for Your Bottom Line," U.S. Commercial Service webpage, http://www.trade.gov/cs/factsheet.asp.

CHAPTER 5

1. Susan Sorenson and Keri Garman, "How to Tackle U.S. Employees' Stagnating Engagement," Gallup News, June 11, 2013, http://www.gallup.com/businessjournal/162953/tackle-employees-stagnating-engagement.aspx.

2. Enron, "Code of Ethics," July 2000, Archived at U.S. Justice Department website, https://www.justice.gov/archive/enron/exhibit/02-06/BBC-0001/ocr/EXH012-02970%5EFullText.TXT.

3. Kris Duggan, "Why The Annual Performance Review Is Going Extinct," FastCompany, October 20, 2015, https://www.fastcompany.com/3052135/why-the-annual-performance-review-is-going-extinct.

4. Charles Duhigg, "What Google Learned From Its Quest to Build the Perfect Team," *The New York Times Magazine*, February 25, 2016, https://www.nytimes.com/2016/02/28/magazine/what-google-learned-from-its-quest-to-build-the-perfect-team.html.

5. David Rock and Heidi Grant, "Why Diverse Teams Are Smarter," *Harvard Business Review*, November 4, 2016, https://hbr.org/2016/11/why-diverse-teams-are-smarter.

6. Ibid.

7. Vivian Hunt, Dennis Layton, and Sara Prince, "Why Diversity Matters," McKinsey & Company, January 2015, http://www.mckinsey.com/business-functions/organization/our-insights/why-diversity-matters.

8. David Rock and Heidi Grant, "Why Diverse Teams Are Smarter."

9. Javier E. David, "Mr. Incredible? Steelers linebacker vows to return kids' 'participation trophies,'" CNBC, August 16, 2015, http://www.cnbc.com/2015/08/16/steelers-linebacker-vows-to-return-kids-participation-trophies.html.

10. Linda Ray, "Employee Turnover Statistics in Restaurants," Houston Chronicle, http://smallbusiness.chron.com/employee-turnover-statistics-restaurants-16744.html.

11. Paul Nunes and Tim Breene, "Reinvent Your Business Before It's Too Late," *Harvard Business Review*, January-February 2011, https://hbr.org/2011/01/reinvent-your-business-before-its-too-late.

12. "20 Years Inside the Mind of the CEO . . . What's Next?" PwC, http://www.pwc.com/us/en/ceo-survey/finding-trust.html.

13. Zach Bulygo, "Tony Hsieh, Zappos, and the Art of Great Company Culture," Kissmetrics Blog, February 26, 2013, https://blog.kissmetrics.com/zappos-art-of-culture/.

14. James Covert, "Blue Apron's Busy New Jersey Facility a Real Fight Club," *New York Post*, October 11, 2016, http://nypost.com/2016/10/11/blue-aprons-busy-new-jersey-facility-a-real-fight-club/.

15. Sage Lazaro, "The Truth Behind Blue Apron: Violence, Health Violations and Impossible Work Demands," *Observer*, October 3, 2016, http://observer.com/2016/10/the-truth-behind-blue-apron-violence-health-violations-and-impossible-work-demands/.

16. Megan Rowe, "David Novak: Leaders Must Recognize and Praise Their Teams," *Nation's Restaurant News*, October 31, 2016, http://www.nrn.com/workforce/david-novak-leaders-must-recognize-and-praise-their-teams.

17. Caroline Winter, "The TEDification of Corporate America," Bloomberg, January 2, 2014, https://www.bloomberg.com/news/articles/2014-01-02/ted-talks-customized-for-corporate-america.

18. Carmine Gallo, "Southwest Airlines Motivates Its Employees with a Purpose Bigger Than a Paycheck," *Forbes*, January 21, 2014, https://www.forbes.com/sites/carminegallo/2014/01/21/southwest-airlines-motivates-its-employees-with-a-purpose-bigger-than-a-paycheck/#634287dd5376.

19. Jack Craver, "Most Workers Open to Leaving Their Jobs," Benefits Pro, July 27, 2016, http://www.benefitspro.com/2016/07/27/most-workers-open-to-leaving-their-jobs.

20. Brian Chesky, "Don't F--k Up the Culture," Medium, April 20, 2014, https://medium.com/@bchesky/dont-fuck-up-the-culture-597cde9ee9d4#.nipzu7tk5.

CHAPTER 6

1. Mary C Lamia Ph.D., "Like it Or Not, Emotions Will Drive the Decisions You Make Today," *Psychology Today*, December 31, 2010, https://www.psychologytoday.com/blog/intense-emotions-and-strong-feelings/201012/it-or-not-emotions-will-drive-the-decisions-you.

2. "McDonald's Coffee Beats Starbucks, Says Consumer Reports," *The Seattle Times*, February 2, 2007, http://www.seattletimes.com/business/.mcdonalds-coffee-beats-starbucks-says-consumer-reports/.

3. Ernan Roman, "The Damage Brands Suffer From Breaking Promises," *Huffington Post*, October 21, 2016, http://www.huffingtonpost.com/ernan-roman/the-damage-brands-suffer-_b_8348396.html.

4. Michael Krigsman, "Bridging the Gap Between Brand Promise and Customer Experience," Beyond IT Failure, ZDNet, June 1, 2014,

http://www.zdnet.com/article/bridging-the-gap-between-brand-promise-and-customer-experience/.

5. Natasha D. Smith, "Ace Hardware's Brand Promise Is Its Strongest Marketing Tool," DMN, March 6, 2015, http://www.dmnews.com/marketing-strategy/ace-hardwares-brand-promise-is-its-strongest-marketing-tool/article/401926/.

6. "The Real Value in Voice-of-the-Customer? The Customer Experience," Mcorp.cx, http://www.mcorpcx.com/articles/the-real-value-in-voice-of-the-customer-the-customer-experience.

7. "Voice Of the Customer (VOC)," Dictionary, Six Sigma website, https://www.isixsigma.com/dictionary/voice-of-the-customer-voc/.

8. "The Real Value in Voice-of-the-Customer? The Customer Experience," Business for You, April 3, 2016, http://business-5u.blogspot.com/2016/04/the-real-value-in-voice-of-customer.html.

9. Mindi Chapel, "Brand Strategy, Data and Customer Experience Are Marketers' New Priorities," *Marketing Week*, May 9, 2016, https://www.marketingweek.com/2016/05/09/importance-of-brand-strategy-data-and-customer-experience-have-grown-at-highest-rate-for-marketers/.

10. John Koetsier, "2M Facebook Fans Better Than Super Bowl Ad, Celeb Endorsement . . . or Twitter Followers," VB, May 6, 2013, https://venturebeat.com/2013/05/06/2m-facebook-fans-better-than-super-bowl-ad-celeb-endorsement-or-twitter-followers/.

11. Amity Kapadia, "40+ Word-of-Mouth Marketing Statistics That You Should Know," Ambassador website, December 30, 2015, https://www.getambassador.com/blog/word-of-mouth-marketing-statistics.

12. Craig Giammona, "In Social Media Marketing, the Burger King Has It His Way," Bloomberg Businessweek, October 1, 2015, https://www.bloomberg.com/news/articles/2015-10-01/burger-king-s-social-media-marketing-is-a-cost-effective-champ.

13. Michael Noice, "What You Need to Know to Improve Your Content Marketing," Entrepreneur, https://www.entrepreneur.com/article/278942.

14. Hayley Peterson, "Why Chick-fil-A Is Beating Every Other Fast-food Chain in the US," *Business Insider*, October 4, 2016, http://www.businessinsider.com/why-chick-fil-a-is-so-successful-016-10.

15. Made in Mars Amazon front end, https://www.amazon.com/gp/aw/sp.html?mp=&oid=&s=A39AIF0WOXNAV8&t=about-seller.

16. Bank of America, "Client Profile," Small Business Owner Report, Fall, 2016, p. 11, http://newsroom.bankofamerica.com/files/press_kit/additional/Small_Business_Owner_Report_-_Fall_2016.pdf.

17. Ibid.

18. Adam Toren, "The Top 6 Small-Business Trends on the Rise," https://www.entrepreneur.com/article/270045.

19. Yuyu Chen, "The Rise of 'Micro-influencers' on Instagram," Digiday, April 27, 2016, https://digiday.com/marketing/micro-influencers/.

CHAPTER 7

1. Christian Caminiti, "Understanding Innovation: How Businesses Adopt New Technology," *Business News Daily*, July 16, 2015, http://www.businessnewsdaily.com/8199-innovation-technology-adoption.html.

CHAPTER 8

1. Paul Leinwand and Cesare Mainardi, "Why Can't Kmart Be Successful While Target and Walmart Thrive?" *Harvard Business Review*, December 15, 2010, https://hbr.org/2010/12/why-cant-kmart-be-successful-w.
2. Davey Alba, "Apple Doesn't Sell All the Phones. But It Makes All the Money," *Wired*, July 13, 2015, https://www.wired.com/2015/07/apple-doesnt-sell-phones-makes-money/.
3. Michael V. Marn, Eric V. Roegner, and Craig C. Zawada, "The Power of Pricing," *McKinsey Quarterly*, February 2003, http://www.mckinsey .com/business-functions/marketing-and-sales/our-insights/the-power-of-pricing.
4. Michael V. Marn, Eric V. Roegner, and Craig C. Zawada, "Pricing New Products," *McKinsey Quarterly*, August 2003, http://www.mckinsey .com/business-functions/marketing-and-sales/our-insights/pricing-new-products.
5. Elizabeth L. Axelrod, Helen Handfield-Jones, and Timothy A. Welsh, "War for Talent, part two," McKinsey & Company, 2001, http://www .andersonpeoplestrategies.com/sites/default/files/uploads/McKWarfor-TalentArticle.pdf.

INDEX

ABOUT THE AUTHORS

SUSAN SOLOVIC

A woman of many talents, Susan Wilson Solovic is an award-winning serial entrepreneur; *New York Times, Wall Street Journal*, Amazon.com top 100, and *USA Today* bestselling author; media personality; sought-after keynote speaker; and attorney.

An Internet pioneer, Solovic was the CEO and cofounder of one of the first video-based Internet sites, a company she grew from its infancy to a million-dollar-plus entity. In 2006, she accepted the Stevie Award (the Oscars of business) on behalf of the company for the Most Innovative Company under 100 employees. That same year, the company was voted the Best Investment Opportunity at a Venture Forum in Silicon Valley.

A media personality, Solovic is a former small-business contributor for ABC News and host of a syndicated radio program, *It's Your Biz.* She appears regularly as a small-business expert on Fox Business, Fox News, *The Wall Street Journal's* "Lunch Break," MSNBC, CNN, CNBC, and many other networks across the country. She hosted her own PBS special, *Reinvent Yourself Now: Become Self-Reliant in an Unpredictable World.* In addition to television and radio appearances, Solovic is a featured blogger on numerous sites, including Constant Contact, Entrepreneur.com, Huffington Post, Sage Advice, AT&T Business Circle, NewsMax TV, and FoxBusiness.com.

MoneyTransferComparison.com recognized Solovic with a 2015 Business Excellence Award, and Dun & Bradstreet Credibility Corporation named her one of its 2015 Top Small Business Influencers. Solovic was also named in the Top 10 of both SAP's Top 51 Potential Human Influencers, and she consistently ranks in the top 5 of the Top 100 Small Business Experts to Follow on Twitter. She has written four bestselling books that have been translated into multiple languages.

In addition to running her business, Solovic serves as a special advocate with the Small Business & Entrepreneurship Council, an advocacy, research, education, and networking organization dedicated to protecting small business and promoting entrepreneurship. For more than twenty years, the council has worked to strengthen the ecosystem for small-business success.

Solovic received the Institute for Women's Entrepreneurship Leader of Distinction Award, and she was the first recipient of AT&T's Innovator of the Year Award for being a pioneer in a new industry. Additionally, she has won numerous awards for small business journalism, including recognition from the U.S. Small Business Administration.

Solovic is a member of the advisory board for the Center for Entrepreneurship at the John Cook School of Business, Saint Louis University, where she also served as an adjunct professor on entrepreneurship in the M.B.A. program. She served on the National Women's Business Council, which counsels the president, Congress, and the Small Business Administration on issues affecting women business owners. She is a past board member of the Women's Leadership Board at Harvard University, the Women Presidents' Organization, Women Impacting Public Policy, and the Institute for the Economic Development of Women.

Solovic began her career as a news anchor and reporter. As a corporate executive, she rose to the C-suite level of a Fortune 100 company, becoming the first female in the company's financial services division. She obtained a law degree from Saint Louis University and is of counsel with the firm Junge & Mele LLP in New York City.

RAY MANLEY

Ray Manley is a writer, online marketer, and occasional jazz musician in Nashville. His professional life is extremely varied: He has worked in Silicon Valley start-up projects; run an e-commerce company; owned and operated a motel; written, edited, and merchandised catalogs; and published a weekly newspaper.